MW00884093

REAL MEN HUG PORCUPINES

A Relationship Toolbox for Men

by

Randy Allsbury

with insights from

Dr. Jim A. Talley

ISBN-13: 978-1470076658

Expert Publishing & Marketing, LLC

www.allsbury.com

Real Men Hug Porcupines

TABLE OF CONTENTS

Chapter   **Page**

Dedication

Thank you to my sweet wife for allowing God to work on me over the years. Thank you for not giving up on me.

Thank you Jim and Joyce Talley for investing in my family.

Thank you Sid and Mary Allsbury (my parents) and Bill and Vinita Park (Sherri's parents) for your incredible example and support.

Thank you Roy and Pennie Williams for giving me "permission" to write, making it possible to spend time with the late J. Keith Miller and for teaching me *"If it's worth doing, it's worth doing badly!"*

Thank you Greg & Suzanne Grimaud and Greg & Rhonda Gunn for being cheerleaders on many levels!

Warning...

This book is written to and for **men** *who claim to be followers of Jesus Christ.*

If you are a Christian and are offended by something I said, you probably needed to hear it.

If I have offended you and you do not claim to be a follower of Jesus Christ, I was not talking to you.

Real Men Hug Porcupines

Introduction

For the past 10 years, Dr. Jim A. Talley has been my pastor, my marriage counselor, and my friend. I met him in June of 2000. I had been in the ministry as a youth minister and minister for about twelve years. For the last five of my ministry years, my wife Sherri had been trying to communicate to me that we needed more income and if it were up to her, we would just have normal jobs and raise our family. We had four kids back then. Ashley was 14, Austin was 10, Avery was 7, and sweet Amy was 3. Sherri and I not only came from Christian families, we were both PK's (preacher's kids).

There is a joke that is a massive exaggeration, but true enough to be funny. It goes like this, "Show me a preacher's kid and I'll show you a mess. Show me a missionary's kid and I'll show you a REAL mess." I was a missionary's kid for almost a decade before becoming a preacher's kid. In truth, only about 20% of MK's and PK's are really messed

"Real men don't walk away from their wives. Real men embrace their wives and deal with whatever issue is facing the relationship."

up. (My opinion.)

The last church I pastored was in a town of about 800 people in the middle of Oklahoma, USA. The first Sunday I preached at that church September 14th, 1997, there were 35 people in attendance. Six of them were my family. Over the next three years our little church grew to a consistent 120 in weekly attendance. We re-covered the pews, put a new ceiling in the sanctuary, and built a new multi-purpose building with a gym, more classrooms and a new kitchen.

I felt pretty good about my life and career even though I was over-weight, had severe sleep apnea, and struggled with depression. My wife Sherri would ask me questions every now and then about our future and what my plan was to provide better or more for our family. My pay from the church was $400.00 a week, plus housing. I also drove a school bus to earn extra money, even though we never had extra money. Every now and then she would talk about a career change for us, but I would quickly throw a cold blanket on that conversation and get us back on track doing "God's" work.

Wednesday, April 19, 2000 a widow lady from the church invited us out to her farmhouse for tea. Sherri and I sat and visited with her for a few minutes, when she pulled out a yellow legal pad and began reading off seven hand-written pages of why my sweet Sherri was a terrible preacher's wife. Instead of defending my wife from these attacks, I kept my "pastor hat" on. With my arm around my wife, I reassured the widow lady that we would work on these things. One of which was that my wife mowed our lawn in a bikini. (It was more like shorts and a tank-top.) She berated my wife for not being friendly to her on Sundays and a few other dagger filled nuggets.

Sherri had seen her parents experience quite a bit of pain and betrayal at the hands of church people. We personally felt betrayed by people in the last church we were at. There we were, once again trying to do good and still managing to be attacked by the ones we were serving.

We went home and Sherri was in tears for a few days. At the end of that week she told me she was resigning from her unpaid music ministry role in the church. Another week went by and she started smoking. After a few weeks, she applied for a job in the nearby city. Sherri found some new friends and got involved in a new music outlet. She started singing karaoke in bars and learned she liked Margaritas.

After the shotgun blast to her heart from the widow lady, Sherri made some new resolutions in her life. She came to the realization she could not please the church people, she could not please her husband, and she could not please God. So, she quit trying. From that point on, my sanguine wife decided to make money and have fun. She did, or at least that's what it looked like from my vantage point.

I began to seek counsel on how to get my wayward wife back on track. Sherri's uncle Roger had told me about a guy named Dr. Talley. I had sent a few people from my congregation to him for marriage help. My marriage was heading south fast, so I decided to make an appointment and take my wife in for a tune-up and a straightening out.

It was mid to late June of 2000 when my wife agreed to go to counseling with me. I needed him to straighten her out because her behavior was starting to affect my ministry. We talked to Dr. Talley for about 45 minutes and when our time for that session was up, he looked at me and said. "Mister, it's time for you to get your priorities in order, or this sweet lady will end up killing herself."

What!!??? Me and my priorities!!??? What about her and her priorities!!??? He said more, "She is behaving normally for someone who has been beaten up and abused by the church and people who are supposed to protect her!"

I was very quiet and angry for the next few minutes. I then asked him what I was supposed to do.

Dr. Talley said, "It's simple: you have to get a grip on your priorities. Get out of the ministry until you can do paid ministry without damaging your family."

It was a Tuesday morning. Without too much thinking on my part, called my church board and asked them to meet me at the building that night. Two out of three elders and three out of four deacons met me that evening. I ripped off the "Band-Aid" in the first five minutes, letting them know I was giving them 30 days' notice. The assumption was, that I was offered a bigger, better ministry somewhere else. They asked me where I was going to be moving. I told them I had no idea, but would be moving into the city in 30 days.

I was surprised and affirmed by their response. They didn't mean any harm. In fact, I believe they had good intentions when they told me they knew my wife was acting irrationally and I was welcome to continue being their pastor even if I got a divorce. They were and are good men but were clearly more interested in the growth of the church than the saving of my wife and family. For the next 30 days I walked through life with blinders on and made it through life one day at a time. The next thing I knew, I was working as a waiter at a seafood restaurant and driving a school bus in Edmond, Oklahoma.

Over the next three years things got much worse before they got better. When I followed Dr. Talley's advice, things would get better. When I ignored his advice, things got worse. The best thing he told us was, "Relationship growth and improvement always feels, three steps forward and two steps back. The two back steps always *feel* straight down. The enemy wants you to give up. Even though the two steps back feels straight down, don't give up."

It's been over a decade since Sherri and I made our first appointment with Dr. Talley. God has blessed our family and marriage in many ways. This has caused me to have hope for any couple and any marriage, no matter how badly they *feel* things are.

About two years ago I started talking to Dr. Talley about the principles and tools he gives husbands and wives to help them find the love and passion they once had for each other. I told him I saw the Pareto Principle (80-20 principle) in the husband-wife relationship. My point was that ladies come more natural to relationships. They get it 80% right out of the gate and men get it 20% out of the gate. He said I was close; it's more like 95% and 5%. We had a good laugh and a few minutes later I asked him if he had ever considered writing a "relationship 101" book for men. At that time he had seven books published in nine languages. He felt it would never sell because as a rule men don't buy relationship books.

I let another year go by and in the summer 2010 approached him one more time. This book is what we came up with. If you are the wife, don't force it on your man. Just pray for him and be patient. You are 95% better prepared for this stuff than he is.

In this book I share our story and give basic relationship principles you need to know. Each chapter offers specific tools you can implement to improve your number one human relationship.

REAL MEN HUG PORCUPINES? What's the title of the book about?

Sherri and I had been married about five years. I had been home from work long enough to get into an argument with her. We were both standing in the kitchen arguing about whatever young couples do.

The verbal volleys went back and forth. The intensity of our discussion kept getting hotter. Anger started to escalate when Sherri burst into tears and said, "It would help if you would just come over here and hug me!"

As a young, stupid male, I had an angry response, "I don't hug porcupines!" I walked out of the house and took a walk to cool down. I didn't get very far down the street when I heard a voice in my head say, "Yes, you do. *Real men hug porcupines.*"

Real men don't walk away from their wives. Real men embrace their wives and deal with whatever issue is facing the relationship.

I cut back through our yard, walked in the back door into the kitchen and hugged my porcupine. When I did, her quills disappeared. Turns out they weren't really quills. They were fears and insecurities we needed to talk about and turn over to God, together.

Chapter One

For Followers of Christ

Let's be clear about something. This book is for men who claim to be Christ followers. The assumption on my part is that you care what the Bible says and what God's will for your life is.

Nailing down your number one relationship, first.

In Craig Groeschel's book, *Going All the Way: Preparing for a Marriage That Goes the Distance,* he talks about focusing on your number one relationship before you start focusing on the number two relationship. In other words, make sure you have shored up your relationship with Jesus Christ before you start thinking about a girlfriend or wife.

Before we go any further, do you understand that God doesn't want religious robots doing church activities and trying to be "good, Christian people". Our God knew you when you were in your mother's womb. He knows you now and he loves

> *"God doesn't want religious robots, doing church activities and trying to be 'good, Christian people'."*

you. He created you a specific way and wants to have a relationship with you.

He created the world and animals and then he created man. He gave man the ability to embrace him or reject him. If you have a family and children, you know your children have the same ability. Your kids can embrace you and honor you or they can ignore you and walk away. We parents all prefer the former, not the latter. I once heard Roy H. Williams say, "God created 'mini-mes' with the ability to say 'NO!'" God loves His entire creation, including the angels, but for some reason he has a special love for us. I think it's because we have the ability to say YES to him and he loves it when we do. "Angels, however, have limitations compared to man, particularly in future relationships. Angels are not created in the image of God, therefore, they do not share man's glorious destiny of redemption in Christ. At the consummation of the age, redeemed man will be exalted above angels (1 Cor. 6:3)." "Kindred Spirit," a magazine published quarterly by Dallas Theological Seminary, summer 1995, pp. 5-7.

Believe it or not, God is right now pursuing a relationship with you. As a matter of fact all of heaven rejoices every time a person down here commits his or her life to Christ. *"I tell you, there is rejoicing in the presence of the angels of God over one sinner who repents." (Luke 15:10, cf. vs.7)*

One of my favorite Christian song writers is a guy named Larry Bryant. Read the following lyrics to

Larry's song called "THAT'S WHEN THE ANGELS REJOICE!"

AT THE COMPLETION OF THE GOLDEN GATE
NO, THE ANGELS DID NOT CELEBRATE
AND WHEN THE WRIGHT BOYS FLEW THEIR BIRD
NO ANGELIC SHOUTS WERE HEARD
THERE'S ONLY ONE THING THAT WE'RE SURE ABOUT
THAT CAN MAKE THOSE ANGELS JUMP AND SHOUT
IT'S WHEN A SINNER MAKES THE LORD HIS CHOICE
THAT'S WHEN THE ANGELS REJOICE

NOW WHEN THE LIGHT BULB FIRST LIT UP THE TOWN
NO, THE ANGELS DID NOT DANCE AROUND
AND WHEN THE MAN STEPPED ON THE MOON

THEY DIDN'T SING A VICTORY TUNE
THERE'S ONLY ONE THING THAT WE'RE SURE ABOUT
THAT CAN MAKE THOSE ANGELS JUMP AND SHOUT
IT'S WHEN A SINNER HEEDS THE SAVIOR'S VOICE
THAT'S WHEN THE ANGELS REJOICE

NOW HEAVEN DOESN'T STRIKE UP THE BAND
FOR ANY OLD OCCASION AT HAND
IT'S GOT TO BE A SPECIAL THING
TO MAKE THOSE ANGELS SING
NOW WHEN THE MODEL T FIRST HIT THE STREET
IT DIDN'T BRING ALL HEAVEN TO ITS FEET
AND WHEN THE FIRST COMPUTER WAS BORN
THEY DIDN'T BLOW OLD GABRIEL'S HORN
THERE'S ONLY ONE THING THAT WE'RE SURE ABOUT
THAT CAN MAKE THOSE ANGELS JUMP AND SHOUT
IT'S WHEN A SINNER MAKES THE LORD HIS CHOICE
THAT'S WHEN THE ANGELS REJOICE

NOW WHEN THE UNITED STATES BECAME A NATION
THERE WAS NO ANGELIC CELEBRATION
BUT ONE LOST SINNER COMES BACK HOME
THEY DANCE FOR JOY AROUND GOD'S THRONE

17

It may sound funny, but that song puts some things into perspective regarding how God feels about you. He has made it clear: He loves you and me and wants to have a relationship with us. In fact, He wants to spend eternity with us, that is crazy, but true.

The first step in nailing down your spiritual base is a simple question: "If you died tonight, where would the real you, your soul, spend eternity?" Are you sure?

Chapter 2

FOCUS ON YOURSELF (Fix You, Not Her)

How then should we live?

How should we live as husbands, fathers, and men?
Ephesians chapter 5 has a lot to say about that. Let's read
it together. It speaks to the ladies also, but let's ignore
that part and focus on ourselves.

Ephesians 5 (The Message)
[1-2]*Watch what God does, and then you do it, like children
who learn proper behavior from their parents. Mostly what
God does is love you. Keep company with him and learn a
life of love.*

*Observe how
Christ loved us.
His love was not
cautious but
extravagant. He
didn't love in
order to get
something from
us but to give
everything of
himself to us.
Love like that.*
[3-4]*Don't allow
love to turn into*

***"Husbands, go all out in
your love for your wives,
exactly as Christ did for
the church—a love
marked by giving, not
getting. Christ's love
makes the church whole.
His words evoke her
beauty." Ephesians 5:25***

19

lust, setting off a downhill slide into sexual promiscuity, filthy practices, or bullying greed. Though some tongues just love the taste of gossip, those who follow Jesus have better uses for language than that. Don't talk dirty or silly. That kind of talk doesn't fit our style. Thanksgiving is our dialect.
⁵You can be sure that using people or religion or things just for what you can get out of them—the usual variations on idolatry—will get you nowhere, and certainly nowhere near the kingdom of Christ, the kingdom of God.
⁶⁻⁷Don't let yourselves get taken in by religious smooth talk. God gets furious with people who are full of religious sales talk but want nothing to do with him. Don't even hang around people like that.
⁸⁻¹⁰You groped your way through that murk once, but no longer. You're out in the open now. The bright light of Christ makes your way plain. So no more stumbling around. Get on with it! The good, the right, the true—these are the actions appropriate for daylight hours. Figure out what will please Christ, and then do it.
¹¹⁻¹⁶Don't waste your time on useless work, mere busywork, the barren pursuits of darkness. Expose these things for the sham they are. It's a scandal when people waste their lives on things they must do in the darkness where no one will see. Rip the cover off those frauds and see how attractive they look in the light of Christ. Wake up from your sleep, Climb out of your coffins; Christ will show you the light! So watch your step. Use your head. Make the most of every chance you get. These are desperate times!
¹⁷Don't live carelessly, unthinkingly. Make sure you understand what the Master wants.
¹⁸⁻²⁰Don't drink too much wine. That cheapens your life. Drink the Spirit of God, huge draughts of him. Sing hymns instead of drinking songs! Sing songs from your heart to Christ. Sing praises over everything, any excuse for a song to God the Father in the name of our Master, Jesus Christ.

Relationships

[21]Out of respect for Christ, be courteously reverent to one another.

[22-24]~~Wives, understand and support your husbands in ways that show your support for Christ.~~ The husband provides leadership to his wife the way Christ does to his church, not by domineering but by cherishing. ~~So just as the church submits to Christ as he exercises such leadership, wives should likewise submit to their husbands.~~

[25-28]Husbands, go all out in your love for your wives, exactly as Christ did for the church—a love marked by giving, not getting. Christ's love makes the church whole. His words evoke her beauty. Everything he does and says is designed to bring the best out of her, dressing her in dazzling white silk, radiant with holiness. And that is how husbands ought to love their wives. They're really doing themselves a favor—since they're already "one" in marriage.

[29-33]No one abuses his own body, does he? No, he feeds and pampers it. That's how Christ treats us, the church, since we are part of his body. And this is why a man leaves father and mother and cherishes his wife. No longer two, they become "one flesh." This is a huge mystery, and I don't pretend to understand it all. What is clearest to me is the way Christ treats the church. And this provides a good picture of how each husband is to treat his wife, loving himself in loving her, and ~~how each wife is to honor her husband~~.

Read this chapter over and over, focusing on the parts applying to you.

There are three reasons I believe the Bible is the Word of God. First is scientific foreknowledge. Second are fulfilled prophecies. Third, the Bible, both Old and New Testaments, changes the heart of man for good.

When we meditate on God's word, it changes us for the better.

Please spend some time meditating and even memorizing all or parts of Ephesians chapter 5. More than anything else, this will help you become the husband and father you are called to be.

Chapter 3

Relationships take time...

A recurring truth you will hear woven through this book is that RELATIONSHIPS TAKE TIME. Real, healthy relationships require an investment of time. No matter the relationship, the more time we spend in it, it gets better and goes up. The less time we spend in it, it gets worse and goes down.

I am a marketing guy. Much of my career is thanks to Dr. Talley. After he encouraged me to get out of the paid ministry in the summer of 2000, he asked a friend of his to give me a shot at selling advertising at a news-radio station in Oklahoma City. Steve was the general sales manager for the station. He took me to lunch and within 15 minutes offered me a job in sales. My first reaction was, "No thank you, I don't care much for salespeople and I don't want to be one." He then offered me a six month guarantee for more money than I had ever made. That

"Real effective business doesn't run on sales or money. The real currency of business is relationships."

meant I would be paid even if I didn't sell anything. At the time I was driving an Edmond, Oklahoma school bus from 6 a.m. to 9 a.m., waiting tables at Pelican's Seafood restaurant from 11 a.m. to 2 p.m., back to the bus from 2:30 p.m. to 4:30 p.m. and then back to serving food from 5 p.m. to 10 p.m.

I took the job. At that time my talk radio experience was listening to it in the early 90's. It was a Monday morning in October of 2000 at 8 a.m. It was my first day on the job and my first "corporate America" sales meeting. Three months before this, I was the preacher at a church in a small town in Oklahoma, population 781.

It's interesting what comes to your mind when you are so nervous and you are about to become sick. The Lord reminded me of the faith of my parents. I was born in 1966. My parents, my sister Jodi and I were headed for the mission field in 1967; more specifically, Germany.

Years later in high school I found out my parents, (Sid and Mary Allsbury) left for Germany with two kids, their plane tickets, $200.00 and a pledge of support from a hand full of churches. As a teenager, I asked my dad what gave him the courage to leave everything he knew, having so little resources. My dad's response was simple. He told me he made a deal with God. My dad was willing to go to Germany and preach the Gospel of Jesus Christ, IF his Heavenly Father would go with him and hold his hand every step of the way.

As I walked into the sales meeting at the radio station, I whispered a quick prayer. "Lord, I am leaving the work I have known and am walking into a different world of work. I will do it, but I am going to need you to go with me and hold my hand. I have no idea what I am doing."

Sixty days into my new career, I hadn't sold anything. I was discouraged and was praying God would get me into some other field of work. I went back to the guy who got me into this mess, Dr. Jim A. Talley. I sat across from him in his office in tears telling him how much I hate trying to sell people stuff and I am failing miserably. Dr. Talley smiled, laughed and said, "I have great news for you, Randy. Real effective business doesn't run on sales or money. *The real currency of business is relationships.* The great news is, you do understand relationships and you know how to make solid relationships with people. You just need to get good at making advertising work, and then make friends with people who advertise. The rest will take care of itself." He went on to say if I spend more time with clients, my relationship will go up, if I spent less time, it will go down.

When I got back to the office that day, I was able to sign up for radio sales training with a guy named Chuck Mefford of Light House Communications. (Google him.) I learned how to use radio to make business owners' cash registers ring. I also started learning something Chuck called relational advertising and marketing. (That's for another book and another time.)

All of this reinforced the point that relationships take time. Time with God, time with your wife, time with your kids, time with relatives, time with friends, and time with all others who matter.

Time is our most valuable resource and time is truly the great equalizer of men. Kings, CEOs, presidents, housewives, doctors, lawyers, plumbers, and homeless people all have the same 168 hours per week. If you spend 56 sleeping, you have 112 hours left to invest in relationships and your work.

Chapter 4

Godly Influence

Because it's a journey, we need to have traveling companions on the road with us. I was a youth pastor and pastor for about 12 years. The entire time I never had a good friend. Every now and then my wife would say something about it. She often prayed for me to get one. It was difficult for me, because everyone I knew were church members and I was careful not to talk about what I was feeling and thinking. I didn't want to derail the train by talking too openly about my issues.

Over the past decade my wife's prayers have been answered. She calls them "my two Gregs." I met Greg Gunn in 1997. He was the main speaker at an event we were attending when I was a youth minister in Wichita, Kansas. Four years later I was selling advertising for a news-talk radio station in Oklahoma City. My phone rang and Greg Gunn asked me if I could help him advertise his company on the Dave Ramsey

> *"The entire time I never had a good friend. Every now and then my wife would say something about it. She often prayed for me to get one."*

show. The talk he gave back in 1997 resonated with me and I remembered many of the details. He talked about how we men as business people, in hobbies or in sports have a plan and vision for the future, but when it comes to our families, we have nothing. For some reason we think everything will take care of itself. It does not. About the time he gave that speech, he started a ministry called Family Vision Weekend. He and Mark Naylor created a ministry for married couples to write out a plan for their families and then to live out the plan. Companies have a written Vision, Mission, and Goals. Why can't families? Over the past decade Family Vision Weekend has helped thousands of couples do family on purpose. If this sounds interesting to you, see Family-ID.com.

When Mr. Gunn and I became friends in 2001, I didn't really care for my wife and she didn't care much for me. We did have four kids to raise, so we put up with each other. Greg was a great encouragement to me during this time and helped me focus on the good in my life.

The other Greg's last name is Grimaud. In February of 1995 I was working for an advertising agency at the time and he became one of our clients. A year later I quit, started my own company and he became a client. He became way more, he was and is my closest friend. I didn't know it was possible to tell someone your darkest stuff and he not run for the hills. I never knew what it was like to have a friend come over at 11 p.m. to confess sin and pray and allow me to do the same. I could go on and on about physical, spiritual, and emotional battles he has helped me win. I will save it for another time and simply encourage you to pray the Lord will bless you with friends for this journey. It makes for an easier trip. Heck, it makes the journey fun.

The most important thing that happens when you have a close friend who is also a Christ follower, is the accountability that takes place. Some accountability is planned and some is not. The planned stuff is like when you both agree you will take your families to church every Sunday. It's when you install CovenantEyes.com on your computer so you won't be tempted to visit websites you shouldn't. Planned stuff is when you ask each other questions about priorities. The stuff you don't plan is when you or your friend are getting off course in one area or another and you are there to help each other get back on the right track.

One time I was visiting with one of Greg Grimaud's work associates and discovered Greg had offended him. This guy was very bitter toward Greg and was avoiding him. I know Greg's heart and knew he didn't mean to hurt this guy. The next time I was with Greg, I let him know about the situation. He did the right thing, by humbling himself and asking for forgiveness. Greg has done the same with me. He has helped me with many integrity issues. He has stood by me waiting and expecting the right decisions to be made.

Real Men Hug Porcupines

Chapter 5

The Big "H"

There is a country song by Mark Chesnutt that goes, *"I'm goin' through the Big D and don't mean Dallas. I can't believe what the judge had to tell us, I got the Jeep, she got the palace..."*

To keep the "Big D" away we men have to continually do what Greg and I call the "Big H." The "H" stands for humility. The biggest thing we see and learn from Jesus is how he humbled himself from his seat at the right hand of God, to a manger, to a boy, to a man, to a cross. Ephesians 5 tells us to humble ourselves to our wife the way Jesus did for the church. He gave his life for his bride, the church.

It's not uncommon for Greg to call me or for me to call him and talk about getting ready to face the big "H." In other words, we need to humble ourselves in some way in order to make something right. We don't like the feeling, but Jesus didn't either.

"We need to humble ourselves in some way in order to make something right."

31

I'll talk about a situation with Greg that is funny now, but wasn't at the time. I will let Greg write his own book and he is welcome to talk about my "H" issues. Not long after he got his life and marriage right with God, he and his wife made an agreement regarding money. Neither would ever spend more than $100 without telling the other ahead of time. Well, Greg likes cowboy boots and one fall afternoon he found himself looking at boots at Shepler's Western Wear. I am not going to tell you the amount, but he was looking at a pair of name brand, alligator skin boots. He tried them on and they fit, oohhhh, so nice. It turns out; he had a 30% off coupon, so the boots would be substantially discounted. His impulsive nature knew "it was a sign from God." The coupon meant he was supposed to buy the well-fitting gator boots. Even with the great discount, the new footwear was dramatically more than the $100, agreement he had made with his sweet wife. Greg got back to his office and stared at the boot box on his desk. He opened the box and each boot was in its own beautiful blue velvet bag like, like Crown Royal. Suddenly he realized he was going to have to tell his wife that he totally blew off their spending rule. Greg did what every smart man would do. He hid them at his office… for almost TWO YEARS. He never wore them and even tried to sell them on the Internet, but couldn't get a high enough e-bid. During the second year of hiding, he had forgotten about them. Then he came across them that fall. He knew the only answer was to take a large swig from the "Big H" bottle (humble pie syrup). He came clean with his wife and asked if he could have them for Christmas.

His wife and three kids gave them to him for Christmas and he pretended to be surprised.

We men are thick in the head and we would rather walk across broken glass than humble ourselves and say "I was wrong. Would you please forgive me?" As a kid I remember watching my favorite show, "Happy Days." Arthur Fonzarelli was the coolest guy on the planet. The Fonz did everything right and cool, until that one time he made a mistake and was forced to say he was wrong. I remember him saying, "I was wwrrrr, I was wrrrrrrrrrrrr." He could not say it. The time I find it the most difficult is when I hurt someone but did not mean to; especially when it's one of my kids. My wife has helped me see those times over the years and helped me address them when possible.

If you ever find out you have hurt someone, you need to humble yourself and apologize. Many of us go around doing a lot of damage, maybe not physically, but emotionally, to the very ones we are to love and protect. It should be obvious to all of us that physical abuse is wrong. We have a more difficult time acknowledging emotional abuse.

Years ago when my wife and I were seeing Dr. Talley on a regular basis, he sent me an e-mail and told me to get a book called *The Verbally Abusive Relationship.* It took me two months to buy the book because I was very offended by the suggestion. "I am not abusive on any level, ESPECIALLY VERBALLY!" I took a dose of the big "H" and read enough of the book to understand something. It's not only what you are saying that is abusive, it is **how she receives it**. I am not one to use bad language, not one to yell or scream and not one to berate my wife over an issue. My sweet wife talked to Dr. Talley about how bad I make her feel when I talk to her about any serious issue. Due to issues in her past, she does not have the emotional ability to handle much verbal conflict. What I might consider a healthy, animated verbal exchange, might be devastating to her emotionally. This goes back to taking responsibility for hurting people you didn't "mean" to hurt.

Chapter 6

Trust God

Like I said in the introduction of the book, my sweet wife Sherri and I sat at the widow lady's kitchen table as she served us sweet tea. She then went back into the living room and retrieved a small legal pad. The elderly farm lady sat down and began reading seven handwritten pages of the many reasons my Sherri was a terrible preacher's wife. Instead of protecting my best friend from this torture, I sat next to her with my arm around her and kept my "pastor" hat on. This mixed up lady was shredding my wife and I just sat there listening.

To that point, Sherri had asked me several times over the years if I would consider doing something else for a living. We are both preachers' kids and she had grown weary of living in the church-leadership fishbowl. She also wanted me to get a job that earned more money than preaching and driving a school bus in a rural community. She felt a huge burden of our financial situation and the need to earn money due to my limited

> *"I did exactly what the counselor told me to do. I didn't like it, but I did it. I was also very hurt and upset."*

income and my apathy toward earning more money. At that point I was providing neither relational nor financial security that my wife needed.

The "legal pad list" was the straw that broke my lady's spirit. Sherri is very generous and is a pleaser of mankind. On April 19th of 2000 she realized she could not please the church people, she couldn't please the local school leadership where she worked as the vocal music teacher, she couldn't please her husband, and felt she couldn't please God so she snapped. Sherri resigned from her voluntary job at our church as the worship leader, quit teaching vocal music, got a new job in a neighboring town, and took up smoking cigarettes.

I could work through the first three, but the smoking drove me insane. That's when I called Dr. Jim A. Talley, (marriage counselor) and made an appointment. I had never met him, but had sent a few people from my church to him in the past years. Thirty minutes into our first appointment, he pointed his finger at me and said, ***"You have one option, get out of the ministry right away and get a regular job, or this lady will probably end up killing herself."*** Dr. Talley went on to say, ***"You preachers are almost all alike and have your priorities all messed up!"*** He then told me to call my church board together for a meeting and resign giving thirty days notice.

I did exactly what the counselor told me to do. I didn't like it, but I did it. I was also very hurt and upset. I found myself in the position of the older brother in Jesus' parable of The Prodigal Son.

Luke 15:11-32 (New International Version)
The Parable of the Lost Son
11Jesus continued: "There was a man who had two sons. 12The younger one said to his father, 'Father, give me my share of the estate.' So he divided his property between them.

13"Not long after that, the younger son got together all he had, set off for a distant country and there squandered his wealth in wild living. 14After he had spent everything, there was a severe famine in that whole country, and he began to be in need. 15So he went and hired himself out to a citizen of that country, who sent him to his fields to feed pigs. 16He longed to fill his stomach with the pods that the pigs were eating, but no one gave him anything.

17"When he came to his senses, he said, 'How many of my father's hired men have food to spare, and here I am starving to death! 18I will set out and go back to my father and say to him: Father, I have sinned against heaven and against you. 19I am no longer worthy to be called your son; make me like one of your hired men.' 20So he got up and went to his father.

"But while he was still a long way off, his father saw him and was filled with compassion for him; he ran to his son, threw his arms around him and kissed him. 21"The son said to him, 'Father, I have sinned against heaven and against you. I am no longer worthy to be called your son.[a]'

22"But the father said to his servants, 'Quick! Bring the best robe and put it on him. Put a ring on his finger and sandals on his feet. 23Bring the fattened calf and kill it. Let's have a feast and celebrate. 24For this son of mine

was dead and is alive again; he was lost and is found.'
So they began to celebrate.
[25] *"Meanwhile, the older son was in the field. When he came near the house, he heard music and dancing. [26] So he called one of the servants and asked him what was going on. [27] 'Your brother has come,' he replied, 'and your father has killed the fattened calf because he has him back safe and sound.'*

[28] ***"The older brother became angry and refused to go in. So his father went out and pleaded with him. [29] But he answered his father, 'Look! All these years I've been slaving for you and never disobeyed your orders. Yet you never gave me even a young goat so I could celebrate with my friends. [30] But when this son of yours who has squandered your property with prostitutes comes home, you kill the fattened calf for him!'***

[31] *" 'My son,' the father said, 'you are always with me, and everything I have is yours. [32] But we had to celebrate and be glad, because this brother of yours was dead and is alive again; he was lost and is found.' "*

The older brother was resentful. His little brother took his inheritance early and partied it all away. He abandoned his responsibilities and his family.

My wife was in the process of abandoning me, our kids, our church, her job, and every expectation we had of her. She was running away from her responsibilities and I was staying home, taking care of "my family's farm." My resentment was growing every day, because in my mind we were doing "our Father's work," work we had been called of God to do for the Kingdom.

In this Bible story, the older son had never been taught that relationships with family and his father are more important than what he was doing for him. His little brother was deceived into thinking he could get his needs met out in the world with money, wine, women, and parties.

At a marriage/family seminar I attended a class called: "The Independent Family vs. The Interdependent Family." The main speaker asked a real family from the audience to join him on stage. He had them get into a circle holding hands facing outward first. Then he said, "This is today's Independent family. They may live together in the same house, but they are all getting their basic human needs met outside the family." By that he means the father gets respect and praise at work and playing sports with his buddies. The mother spends hours every week with her friends and her work in relationships and fun. The kids spend more time at their friends' homes than their own and they seek approval from peers instead of family. The speaker then asked the family to make a circle facing inward holding hands. The Interdependent Family works on meeting each other's needs at home. Dad can't wait to get home because his wife and kids are his number one cheerleaders. His wife encourages him and makes him feel like a champion and her knight in shining armor. His kids love to be around him and spend time with him, and he them. The husband makes it clear to his wife she is his Queen and he does everything with her and for her. He spends time with her every day alone, talking to her and helping her know she is his one and only. In this dynamic, the home is the hub of the family wheel and each member is not the hub of their own wheel.

The prodigal son left home to get his needs met. The older brother was getting his needs met though his friends and his work. For some reason no one ever helped them love each other and depend on each other as friends and brothers.

Dr. Talley asked Sherri and me to take a Taylor Johnson Temperament Analysis, (TJTA). That is a test to help you see how you are doing emotionally in about nine different areas. When we got the results back, the truth about my own issues began to surface. Sherri's score indicated she was relatively well balanced and my score told him I was messed up in about 7 of 9 categories. This irritated me as well and this time I decided to fight back. I told him his TJTA analysis was bogus. "I am behaving right, and she is behaving wrong!" He shot right back at me, letting me know Sherri was behaving normally for someone who had been abused by her husband and her church most of her adult life.

I didn't like that either. No one is going to tell me I am an abusive husband. Later when I was alone with him, he explained that verbal and emotional abuse is perceived by the victim as that. It's not what I consider abuse that makes it abuse, but how it is affecting her. He went on to explain that if she grew up in a household where dad never raised his voice and she never saw her parents argue or fight, she would naturally be hyper-sensitive to getting in a fight with her husband. Talley hit that nail on the head. Sherri's parents never fought around her or her brothers. They took a drive or waited for the kids to go to bed before they ever had a "discussion." When we got into our first fight almost 25 years ago, it was devastating to her and deep in her heart she knew in her "knower" that we would probably not make it as a couple.

I had to trust God with most of this information Dr. Talley was giving me. I didn't understand most of what he was talking about at the time, but he seemed to have a better plan for reconciliation than I did, so I followed his advice.

The next months were very difficult for me because our counseling consisted of Dr. Talley helping me to get my priorities in order and letting Sherri do whatever she wanted to do. That's not 100% accurate, but it felt that way to me.

Chapter 7

TOP 5 PRIORITIES

One afternoon at a session we were having, Talley gave me a piece of paper and a pen. He then said, "I am now going to give you your new priorities. Write them down and apply them to everything in your life. Then prioritize your time in the same order." Here they are:

1. God
2. Family
3. Job
4. Ministry
5. Recreation

THE GOD PRIORITY

He told me my first priority is my relationship with God. Then he told me relationships take time. If I want my relationship with God to improve, I must spend time with him. Make it simple, but consistent.

"The way to build a relationship with friends or family is by spending time with them talking about ideas and dreams." - Walt Disney

"God talks to you. You talk to God." He handed me a Bible and asked me to read John 11:35 and then say a short prayer. I looked up the scripture and learned it is the shortest one in the Bible, "Jesus wept." I read it and said a short prayer about my family. "This is the starting point for you. Every day read another verse or passage and then talk to God about whatever is troubling you or about how the scripture spoke to you. That's it. Priorities are more about the importance of consistency than the amount of time you spend. You make a determined effort to consistently read the Bible and pray. You will soon begin knowing the heart and mind of almighty God." We'll dig deeper on this in the chapter designated for the priority of God in your life.

THE FAMILY PRIORITY

Next, make sure you schedule and spend time with your family letting them talk to you and you encouraging them with your words. Under the FAMILY umbrella, your wife comes first, then your kids. Spend consistent one-on-one time with your wife. Walt Disney once said, "The way to build a relationship with friends or family is by spending time with them talking about ideas and dreams." Do the best you can to spend this kind of time with each of your kids also. Your children need to know you are a safe-haven for their words. Encourage them to have hopes and dreams and to talk to you about them. The opposite of hope is despair and the opposite of dreams is the drudgery of status quo. We want our kids to feel safe talking to us about drudgery and despair as well. This can only happen when you consistently spend time with them.

THE JOB PRIORITY

The reason your job is your next priority is because you chose marriage and family. 1 Timothy 5:8 says, "If anyone does not provide for his relatives, and especially for his immediate family, he has denied the faith and is worse than an unbeliever." You have a responsibility as a husband and father to provide for your family's needs. Your job is tied to your family finances. Your career choice also takes a back seat to their needs. We men often define ourselves by our work. It's usually the first thing that comes up in a manly conversation. "What do you do?" You may be fortunate enough to earn enough money doing what you like to do to take care of your family's needs. I'll address this in much more detail as well.

THE MINISTRY PRIORITY

As Christ followers we go through challenging times in our lives. God gives us "Grace-Certificates" or "Comfort Coupons" to help us through these times. It is our role to pass those on to hurting people he puts in our path. I grew up in a generation where we put church activity over all other. Attending worship, Sunday school, Sunday night church, and Wednesday night Bible study took first priority and everything else comes after that. The number one relational priority wasn't with God, it was with the program of the church. Greg Gunn of Family Vision Ministries puts it this way, "You have heard the scripture *Matthew 16:26, What good will it be for a man if he gains the whole world, yet forfeits his soul? Or what can a man give in exchange for his soul?* I can think of something worse. **What good would it be for a man to win the entire world to Christ and lose his own children to darkness?"**

THE RECREATION PRIORITY

This is challenging for me. That is having some kind of consistent healthy recreation. I like fishing, golf, and playing Frisbee golf with my boys, but have a difficult time planning them consistently into my schedule. A lot of time often goes by without me taking time to recreate. A lot of men make this their first priority. The reason it is their first, is because it's what they schedule first, consciously or sub-consciously. If you are wondering about yourself, ask this question. Do you plan your hunting, fishing, golf, or other hobby activities with great detail and forget to have a consistent plan getting your kids to church? Do you always forget your wife's birthday, yet always remember the annual trip to the lake with you buddies? Do you have consistent time for your fun days, but never plan family-fun days? When you are single, you can usually get away with the axis of your world coming down through the middle of your head and exiting your rear end. When you get married, it must shift and when you have kids, it must shift more.

Chapter 8

PRIORITY NUMBER ONE

Making a shift in your priorities is the first step in having your closest relationships succeed. Any decision you are making or any plan you are making should be held up to the new priorities. 1. **GOD** 2. FAMILY 3. JOB 4. MINISTRY 5. RECREATION.

Relationship with God

A farmer and his wife were driving into town to go shopping. As they were driving down the road in their pickup she commented about their relationship. She was sad that they weren't as close as they used to be. She said they used to sit right next to each other all snuggled up and cozy in the truck and nowadays you sit right next to your door and I sit by mine. There was a long pause, and then the farmer said, "I didn't move."

If you don't have the same relationship with God that you did in the past, guess who moved?

I am as guilty as the next person about moving close to God and then away. My buddy, Greg Gunn,

"Is prayer your steering wheel, or your spare tire?"
---Corrie Ten Boom

teaches a lesson on how to become white-hot for Jesus. He describes his relationship with God as lukewarm at best until he was 42 years old. When he is teaching on stage, he has a table lamp with the shade removed in order to see and touch the bulb. He says, "I would like to get this light-bulb really hot, so hot it will burn me if I touch it." Greg plugs the light in and then unplugs it after about five seconds. He plugs it back in and then unplugs it again. After doing this a few times, he unplugs it, waits a few seconds and touches the bulb. "It's just not that hot. Can anyone help me understand why the bulb is not staying hot?" he asks. Someone usually points out the obvious and Greg goes on to compare that to the way his spiritual life used to be. At age 42 Greg decided the reason his walk with God was warm at best was because he was inconsistent at being "connected to the vine."

Like Greg, I believe it is important to write things down. He reads the Bible and journals every day. I do the same, but am inconsistent at times. The key is not getting discouraged with yourself. Another friend of mine only writes in his journal a few times a month. He reads the Bible or a devotional every day, but only writes something in his journal if it is extra meaningful or something he wants to share with his wife and/or kids.

The point is: relationships take consistent time and your relationship with God is no different. You talk to God; God talks to you.

As a Christ-follower, you will be spending eternity with 1 & 2. Make sure they are your first investment.

Make a card for yourself with these priorities on it. Have it laminated and keep it with you.

If you are someone who plans your time, make sure you place things on your calendar in order of priority. It's always not the amount of time you give something that makes it a priority. It is placing it in your schedule and not missing it.

GOD PLANNING

On a daily basis choose a time that will work best for you to talk to God and you allow him to talk to you. You might start by keeping a Bible in the bathroom. Read a Proverb and talk to God about your day, everyday. You might do better on your lunch break every day or you might be a person who can end your day reading a few verses and visiting with God before you go to sleep. You may spend one minute or one hour with God. The issue here is not missing, because you have made it a priority.

Don't make this complicated. This is you setting aside some time every day for you to talk to God and allow him to talk to you. Dr. Talley told me early on that the quality of all relationships rises and falls directly related to time alone spent together. If you are a business man and you play golf every week with one of your clients, your relationship with them and the business you do together is going to be better than the client you visit once a quarter.

I recommend you get a journal or a notebook and write down a few verses you read, a few thoughts the words give you and whatever else you need to talk to God about.

I asked Dr. Talley about this and he said he likes to use the word ACTS as an acronym. (TOOL)

A ---Adoration
C ---Confession
T ---Thanksgiving
S ---Supplication

Adoration: Begin by telling God how much you ADORE Him; reminding yourself who God is. He is the Creator of all things. We are nothing without God making all things happen. Your next breath is dependent on His power.
Confession: Integrity is the time it takes between mess up and fess up. A man of integrity confesses his sins and asks for forgiveness.
Thanksgiving: Thank God for what he is doing for you today and for what he has done for you in the past. That's another reason to journal this stuff. You will be able to look back and read what he has done for you over the years.
Supplication: "Okay, Doc, what does this mean?" Simple: It's asking God for the supplies you need today!

My wife encourages me to take pictures of family events. Why? She says if we don't take pictures, it didn't happen. In the history of the world, it didn't happen if it didn't get written down by someone. If you will write down a few notes of your dialog with God, you will be able to look back and see the hand of God on your life. Your children will find them someday and be able to witness God working in your life and they will be able to tell your grandchildren of God's faithfulness.

Get involved in the local church...

Part of your relationship with God is attending church in corporate worship, making an outside statement of what God is doing in your life. In most cases, that's where we men can develop relationships with other like-minded men who want to be some kind of spiritual leader in their family. We were made for relationships with other people. We need the encouragement of other men. We need to be mentored by other men and we need to mentor the men following us.

You as spiritual leader...

Most of us are intimidated by those words. You may have never had a father who was a spiritual leader and you have no idea what that looks like. The spiritual leader is simply in charge of making sure spiritual things happen in the life of your family. Make sure a prayer happens before meals. You don't have to always be the one who prays, you just make sure it happens. You also plan when and where you and your family are going to attend church. Your wife and kids will thank you some day for taking the lead here.

It's not what you do for God, he doesn't need you. He wants a relationship with you, his son.

We men tend to be a bit task oriented. "Give me my weekly list and let me get it punched out, so I can go fishing or play golf relatively guilt free." Your Heavenly Father wants a relationship with you just like your wife and kids do. You would never consider your family relationships to be a list of tasks you check off every week. When we stop spending time with God every day, He becomes a task master, not a friend and father we do life with.

If you don't have a relationship with God, your kids won't either.

Your kids can handle you making mistakes, losing your cool, arguing with your wife, and allowing them to see whatever weaknesses you have. They can't handle you being a phony in your relationship with God. The sermon you live will tell them where God is in your life. They will know if Jesus Christ is part of your hub or just one of many spokes. When problems arise, do you curse God? Or do you press into Him even harder? Do your kids ever catch you reading the Bible? Do they ever walk in on you when you are praying with your wife? Have you ever asked your kids to pray for you about a struggle you are facing?

Corrie Ten Boom once asked a group of people, "Is prayer your steering wheel, or is it your spare tire?"

In 2005 I moved our family into the biggest, most expensive house we had ever lived in based on the income I was making with the company I was working for. Less than thirty days after moving in, I had to walk away from that company. The best thing for me to do at the time was start my own company. I quit October 17th, 2005 and that night I asked my two oldest kids, Ashley and Austin to join me in the living room. She was 19 and he was 16. I told them what had transpired that day and that I was going to start my own company. Tears were running down my cheeks as I told them that this change is much larger than I am. Further, I will be relying 100% on my Lord and Savior to help me. I then asked both of them to pray over me for wisdom as I moved forward. They rarely see their daddy cry, and this was a time for me to demonstrate my belief that I might not have what it takes, but I know my Daddy in Heaven does and he wants me to lean on him every day. When you leave a job or career, there is a part of every man that feels like a bit of a failure. We men don't want to walk away from any battle. We want to win. I once read a quote attributed to Mother Teresa when asked by a reporter if she ever fails at anything. She said, "Yes, of course. I call my failures 'the kisses of Jesus.' It's only in my failures I am forced to go running into the arms of my Savior."

After we lost our home and belongings to a fire in November of 2003, my son Avery was sitting in his Sunday School class at Edmond Christian Church, in Edmond, OK. Avery was ten years old and his teacher said, "I am sorry about your family losing your home to the fire. I bet your parents are really worried." Without even lifting his head up from his craft project he said, "My parents don't worry, they pray." The truth is,

Sherri and I were very worried about what we were going to do, but what Avery saw was parents who lean into God in prayer during everyday life.

Your relationship with God is your first priority and your wife and kids need to catch you working on this relationship. I heard a guy say, "If it's worth doing, it's worth doing BADLY." He meant no one hits a home run the first time up to bat. No one shoots par in their first round of golf. When we start something new in our lives, we usually do it badly in the beginning. My first book was an audio book with printed transcript. My second was a self-published version of my blog writings. My third book is still in my computer in a file folder. This is my fourth attempt and it's worth doing badly. Dr. Talley helped me by encouraging me to write and not edit. "You're just the writer. Someone else will edit it and make it pretty for you."

We men don't like to start anything we are uncertain of winning or doing perfectly. Your daily conversations with God are your business and no one else's. He doesn't check for spelling or grammar. He wants to be involved in every area of your life.

Make your first priority in life your relationship with God.

Chapter 9

PRIORITY NUMBER TWO

1. GOD 2. **FAMILY** 3. JOB 4. MINISTRY 5. RECREATION.

It's not the amount of time you spend on each priority. It's the fact you made it a priority that matters. What you give first priority to is your master or your god. You are doing this on purpose or you are letting your schedule prioritize itself. Most of us swerve in and out of this. Sometimes we are intentional with our time and sometimes we let it slide on by without much thought.

If the amount of time we spent on things made it our god or idol, we would have to agree that sleep must be our god. After all, that is what we spend our time doing most consistently. If not sleep, it might be your job. Some people do make their job the number one priority. Most do so because that's where they see their money coming from. I personally believe your job comes from God and He supplies your needs.

"He went on to tell me our town-house apartment caught on fire Thanksgiving Day and burned all night. He was pretty sure it was a total loss."

55

Your second priority is not to earn money. It is to provide safety, security, and spiritual leadership to your wife and children. The average American man shifts his career seven times before he settles in on the one he retires from. That's a long series of leaning your main ladder against the wrong buildings.

When you look at your weekly schedule you will first schedule relationship with God things. You will have a relationship longer with Him than anyone else. Next, you schedule family things, beginning with wife and then your kids.

A.T.A.T. (Accumulated Time Alone Together)

My dad taught me to change the oil on a car when I was 13 years old. If you asked most people why it is important, they would say oil breaks down and must be replaced. That's true but not the whole story. Changing the oil in your car also cleans out the inner workings. Even though your car has an air filter to keep contaminants out, dust and particles still get inside. By the time you have driven your car 3000 to 5000 miles, the oil has gotten thin because all fluids break down and it turns almost black due to all of the contaminants it has trapped in your engine. If you never or rarely change your oil, the heat and friction make the oil less slippery and more watery and the contaminants build up inside your engine until eventually it gunks up all the parts and it seizes up. At that point you have to buy a new engine. Most people have the car hauled to the scrap yard and get a new car.

In the early fall of 2003 I was at a cross-roads regarding my marriage. For two years I tried to do whatever Dr. Talley told me to do regarding the salvation of my marriage and family. My wife had turned a significant corner spiritually but I was tired and didn't really like her. That feeling was mutual. I was sitting on the patient side of Talley's desk and he asked me how much time I spend with her alone. My response was venom-laced sarcasm, "How much time do you spend alone with people you don't care for?" He went on to ask me if I ever change the oil in my car. That's a weird question. He said spending conflict-free time with her alone is like changing the oil on your car. "Ooohhh, I can see that… NOT!" Dr. Talley said all relationships take time. The more time you spend alone talking about ideas, feelings and dreams, the relationship goes up and the less time… it goes down.

Surely it can't be that simple. It turns out, it's true. The more time you spend alone with God every week talking to and listening to Him, the more your walk with Him improves.

Okay, but what about the oil change business?

As you go through life, contaminants and friction cause your insides to get "dirty and cluttered." Talking with a friend about your "stuff" allows them to be released. After they are released, your operating engine moves smoothly again. You and your wife both need this, she needs it more.

Ding, ding, ding… I suddenly began to make some connections from things my dad told me and from things I had heard and read over the years. How many times have you heard people say "You need to listen to her talk. Listen to her problems but don't try to fix them. Just listen."? That never made any sense to me until Dr. Talley gave me another testosterone filled analogy.

"Randy, do you know what an electric capacitor is?" I wasn't sure but said yes because I am a man and knew he was going to explain it anyway. "A capacitor can hold an electric charge, just like a battery, but unlike a battery, a capacitor releases it's entire charge when it's grounded. A battery releases it slowly over time. A battery must be recharged over time. A capacitor can get a full charge immediately or it can get charged up a little bit at a time over time. There is a capacitor mechanism in your car's turn signal blinker. The bulb lights up, a ground wire hits it and it goes back off; over and over and over…

"Randy, your wife is a capacitor. So are you, but right now we are talking about her. As Sherri works her way through life, her capacitor is being charged by stresses. Good and bad stress. Both add electricity. Eventually she reaches maximum 'capacity.' If you are a smart man, and I think you are, you will realize her ground wire runs from her mouth to your ears. As she talks to you about the stresses in your life, the hot voltage is released and peace begins to take over once again."

I was stunned. "So you are saying that every time I interrupt her or try to fix what she is talking about, it prevents the voltage release?"

Talley: "I knew you were smart!"

Me: "So you are saying the only chance I have to save this marriage and family is to become friends with her, by spending time with her."

Talley: "Yes."

I am a right-brained, creative type person who has purchased many calendars over my lifetime and still have no idea how to use one. Planning anything consistently will only happen if I give it top priority and do it every day.

Thursday night November 8th 2003 I asked my wife if she would be interested in splitting a Grand-Slam breakfast with me at Denny's the next morning. She agreed to it and we went. I squeegeed my brain of all possible expectations and did my best to have eggs and bacon with a friend. The time was uneventful, but we agreed to do it again the next morning and the next. I called Dr. Talley and told him I was making a commitment to him to take my wife to breakfast every morning for a year. He laughed and said, Okay.

We went Friday, Saturday, Sunday, Monday, Tuesday…

Tuesday I got fired from my job. My wife had recently quit her job to help me with mine. A voice in my head told me not to be angry with my employer but to trust God because this was an attack of the enemy, Satan. Sherri and I made an appointment to visit an incredible prayer warrior the next night. We spent three hours with him in prayer. It felt like 30 minutes. He encouraged me, "Continue your daily Denny's time together and trust God for new jobs. Your job is not your provider, your Father in Heaven is."

I had $600.00 in the bank and was optimistic about getting work. The next week my mother called from Missouri and reminded me we were doing something different for Thanksgiving. Instead of going to her house, we were all going to spend the holiday in Branson, Missouri at a hotel that had an indoor water-park connected to it. My four kids were excited!

We drove to Branson from our town-house apartment in Edmond, Oklahoma, Wednesday morning November 26th, after Sherri and I did Denny's together. We had $200.00 left and a God who supplies our every need. We had a wonderful time in Branson with my parents, my siblings, their spouses, and kids. It was 28 degrees outside and we had a blast swimming and water-sliding indoors. We used a small hotel conference room for family snacks and games and ate our Thanksgiving meal at a local restaurant. This was nice for my mother. Sherri and I found a Denny's in Branson and continued our ritual.

Our plan was for my family to head to my parents' house on Friday the 28th and spend the rest of the weekend with them. That plan changed early that morning when my brother-in-law, Greg, walked into our hotel room and handed me his cell phone. My cell phone was dead so the pastor of our church called Greg. He asked me if I were sitting down. I laughed and said, "No, I am lying down under my covers…" He went on to tell me our town-house apartment caught on fire Thanksgiving day and burned all night. He was pretty sure it was a total loss.

I called Sherri's dad in Oklahoma City and asked him if he would go check it out and give me an update. Sherri and I went to breakfast and then came back and had a prayer time with my entire family. My father-in-law called and told me to not bother coming back quickly. Our home was charred black inside, was full of water from the fire department and was boarded up with ply-wood.

We first decided to go to my parents for the rest of the weekend. By the time we got there and unloaded the kids, we couldn't stop ourselves from heading home. Five hours later we arrived back in Edmond. It was dark and all power was turned off to our unit. (Firemen are smart.) We went to Wal-Mart and purchased rubber boots and flashlights. Returning to the scene of the fire, I had to get a Phillips head screwdriver out of my trunk to remove the two sheets of plywood covering out back door. The smell to me was of burnt popcorn. When I leaned the wood against the wall, I could not help noticing a large, black, metal looking porcupine thing. It was Sherri's piano. The only thing left was the iron sounding board and broken strings resembling the quills. We stepped into the black, cavernous, cold swamp with our flashlights and felt like we were in some other Twilight Zone time dimension. Sherri shined her light to the floor on the right. "What is that?" It looked like some pipes and wire covered with black and green goo. I laughed. It was our artificial

Christmas tree. She had put up our decorations before we left for Branson so she would not have to do it when we got back. We swung our lights to the other side of the living room and there six black Christmas stockings were still hanging above the bar. I have no Idea what those socks were made of, but they hardly burned at all. My sister-in-law, Stephanie, made those stockings for us the year before. It's funny but that's the only thing that upset my sweet wife that night.

My brother, John, and his wife, Stephanie, lived in Edmond as well and gave us access to their house. We went over there and napped for a few hours. The next morning after staring at each other for thirty minutes over our Grand-Slam breakfast, we went back to Wal-Mart and picked up some cheap sweats to wear while cleaning and salvaging.

A few moments later we were standing in the middle of the toasted mess. Upstairs there was a loft area, two bedrooms and a full bath. The clean white painted walls were all black. The burnt popcorn smell was laced with melted and burning plastic. At the top of the stairs it looked like there was a smear of melted chocolate on the wall. I had no idea what it was until I looked down to see the inner mechanism of the thermostat on the floor. The plastic shell melted down and left the mercury switch and spring intact.

Sherri's cell phone rang. It was her brother, Bert, who was a worship pastor in Joplin, Missouri. She updated him in tears. Bert said, "Remember Sherri, the joy of the Lord is your strength. I love you."

Sherri's father, Bill Park, showed up a few minutes later and helped us start moving forward. That means we started hauling all of our stuff to the six dumpsters located throughout the complex. As Sherri was carrying broken and melted dishes out, a tall African American man approached her and told her how sorry he was about the loss of our belongings. He reached in his pocket and pulled out some cash. "I know this isn't much, but I would really like to help you," he said as he handed $50 to my Sherri. Instinctively, she gave him a gentle stiff-arm and said, "Oh, no thank you, you don't need to do that. We'll be okay." He insisted and my wife realized that we did need the money and she didn't really know if we would be okay. She smiled and thanked him, then turned and began walking back inside. Tears began to flow as she walked back from the dumpster. Her dad embraced her and she told him about the gift and how she did not want to take it. Bill's words were the right ones. "Sherri, that man is being used by God to provide for you and your family. Let him. He is receiving a blessing from giving to you." His words helped prepare us for several months of trusting God and accepting with grace and gratitude the help from His people.

Word was getting out to our friends and about 10:00 a.m. my friend Greg Gunn called. He offered, but there wasn't much he could do to help at the time. He did say something we had already heard that morning. "Remember, the joy of the Lord is your strength!" He added, "A lot of people pray for strength to get through tough times. I encourage you to pray for the joy of the

Lord. He will give you joy and peace in the midst of your anxiety."

I don't remember who it was, but one other person talked to Sherri that day and said, "The joy of the Lord is your strength." Nehemiah 8:10: "Do not grieve, for the joy of the Lord is your strength." Why is joy important?

Because the "joy of the Lord is your strength!" Joy produces strength and the Lord knew we were going to need strength to get through this event.

Still Saturday, around noon my phone rang. It was Greg Gunn's brother, Nathan. He told me how sorry he was and then offered me his house to live in for the next 6-8 weeks. Nathan and his lovely wife, Sally, lead an international ministry called JESUS BOOTH. Nathan felt called into street ministry years ago, but is sort of an introvert and would never consider being one of those annoying Bible thumping, inner city, street preachers. He would however be willing to talk to people about Jesus, if they approached him. One day, a few years earlier, Nathan went to a hardware store and bought a bunch of 1" PVC pipe and parts to hook them together. The first Jesus Booth was created in his garage and a new ministry was born. He took some Bibles and other literature to downtown Oklahoma City that evening and set up a booth, just big enough for him to stand in. He fashioned curtains for it and a sign at the top that simply said, "Do you have questions about Jesus?" Years later, he has built hundreds of these micro-booths and other Jesus Booth ministers are using them in major cities all over the world. (Google Jesus Booth Ministries to see pictures.)

Nathan, Sally, and their toddler, Gabriel, were heading to Los Angeles, California for eight weeks of Jesus Booth ministry. That way they were able to loan us their home.

My family stayed with my brother, John, and his wife, Stephanie, for two weeks, before we headed over to Nathan Gunn's house.

We were still living out of the suit cases we had taken to Branson, Missouri when we moved our tribe of six into the Gunn's house. When we arrived, there was an envelope on the kitchen counter with my name on it. Sally Gunn had told their mail-lady about us staying at their house. The mail-lady gave $60 to Sally to give to "The family that lost everything on Thanksgiving…" We were blown away! That was God providing for us through a person we had never met. That was only the beginning.

A TASTE OF JOY

We moved into Gunn Manor on a Saturday and got up the next morning to go to church. Our kids were still with relatives. It had snowed the night before and was very cold. We got in Sherri's little green Mazda MX3 and started the car. I reached up to turn on the stereo, so we could listen to some praise music on the way to church, but there was a huge hole in the dash where Sherri's very nice car stereo was the night before. By nice I mean Blaupunkt, (Google it). The stereo came with the car and it was awesome. I looked down to the floor-board and the criminal who had stolen our car radio had left his screwdriver behind. Sherri and I looked at each other and began laughing. I said, "OKAY, LORD WE HAVE THE MESSAGE, WE ARE TO RELY ON YOU AND NOT ON OUR EARTHLY, MATERIAL STUFF. WE GET IT." Peace and the joy of the Lord filled us as we laughed about the stolen stereo all the way to church. We did stop by Denny's for breakfast, first.

GOD PROVIDES FOR HIS CHILDREN

While living at Nathan and Sally's house, the complex our townhouse was in had a 3-bedroom apartment come available and the manager offered it to us. We signed a short lease. We had an apartment, but no furnishings, dishes, food, washer or dryer.

We kept the kids going to the same schools and did our best not to change their lives. Our daughter, Amy, was in the first grade. God put it on the hearts of her entire homeroom class to care for our family. It seemed like every other day she came home from school with a Target or Wal-Mart gift card taped to a folder inside her backpack. They ranged from $50 to $200 in value. We learned the only thing you can't do with a Wal-Mart gift card in America, is pay your rent, insurance and utilities! Between Sam's Club, Wal-Mart Stores and Wal-Mart Neighborhood Market, we were covered.

The lady that fired me a couple of weeks before Thanksgiving heard of our plight and sent us $500.00 in

Old Navy gift cards. Sherri enjoyed taking the kids there and buying them clothes.

We began receiving checks in the mail from people in our church, from people at churches we had attended in the past, and from people we had never heard of or met.

One Thursday in early December, we got a call from the Edmond Fire Department. These are the fire fighters that put out our fire. The Fire Chief invited us to come to their station because the men had a few Christmas gifts for our children. That evening we drove to the station. We were warmly greeted and invited in for some hot chocolate and cookies. The men gave us a tour of the station and let our kids climb up in the trucks and play with some of their gear. They gave us a box of gifts for the kids and a home-made envelope of grey construction paper. The envelope was odd and bulky. As we drove home later that night Sherri tore it open and wads of cash fell out on her lap. She counted the ones, fives, tens, twenties, and fifties. The firemen had given us over $1600 in cash out of their own pockets. I had or have since never seen such a spirit of generosity. While there, a fireman give me a card with his name on it. He told me he had a living room pit group he wanted to give to us and all I had to do is come and get it. I did and we used it for three years after the fire. Sherri and I were able to buy a washer and dryer, a dining room table with chairs, and new bedroom suit with a new mattress with the money they gave us.

Two day-care centers and a Boy Scout troop adopted our family as the one to care for that Christmas. One

Saturday morning the first part of December we were asked to visit a local church Boy Scout troop where we were greeted with a large gift bag for each member of our family. The day-care centers did the same and I felt equally awkward loading my car with all the gifts and toys for children.

I walked around in a fog during this time. Every part of me wanted to tell people that we really didn't need any help. I just wanted to say, "No, thank you, we are fine." Inside, I knew the truth, we were not fine and all I could do was "trust in the Lord with all my heart and lean not on my own understanding." Mid December we were still living at the Gunn's house and were slowly putting pieces of furniture in the apartment. The living room still had no furniture, but we had a Christmas tree in the corner and ¾ of the floor covered with gift bags and gifts of all shapes and sizes.

My family in Missouri brought up a pick-up truck load of twin beds for our kids. We were given about a dozen giant trash bags full of clothes, much of which was not the right size, so we passed it on to the Goodwill in town. My two older kids love t-shirts and there was a supply of them to go through.

We set a goal of moving into the apartment the week of Christmas and we did, the weekend before. By then, most of the apartment had furniture. I brought the living room sofa group over from the fireman's house and the living room was totally filled with Christmas gifts. You could see no floor at all and this was five days before Christmas.

Sherri decided it would be a good idea to make some room by allowing the kids to open five (yes *five*) presents a night for the five days leading up to Christmas day. We started this on Saturday the 20th and finalized the event Thursday morning Christmas day.

Only a loving God and Creator of the universe could orchestrate such an incredible celebration of the birth of His Son! The scripture that kept coming into my mind was from the story of Joseph in Genesis chapter 50. Joseph's brothers had sold him into Egyptian slavery and told his father he had been killed by a wild animal. Many years later Joseph ends up as the prime-minister of Egypt with his brothers standing before him asking to buy food from him. Joseph eventually reveals who he is and his brothers cower in fear. In verse 20 of that chapter, He says, "You intended to harm me, but God intended it for good to accomplish what is now being done, the saving of many lives." The same thought was going through my mind. What Satan meant for evil, God used for good on many levels.

The levels…

By burning all of our stuff, we got new stuff. The old stuff had a lot of memories attached to it. New stuff offered us a new start. Sherri and I had just been through a time of relational ugliness. A new setting with new tools gave us a chance to start over.

We were also forced to lean into each other as we leaned into God.

Ashley, Austin, Avery and Amy were able to be witnesses as their parents worked daily on their relationship with each other and with God.

There is a moment in time that still chokes me up as I write this. When Avery expressed confidence in his parents by saying, "My parents don't worry, they pray," he was close. The reason it appeared to my son as though we didn't worry, is because there are times in your life as a follower of Christ that you go way past worry. You reach a point where you finally realize everything is out of your control. It never was IN your control, but at least now you see it as it is. At this point we finally did "let go, and let God." He never leaves us and never forsakes us.

My bride and I continued to go to breakfast every morning together. By that time we were going through a daily devotional book based on Robert McGee's book, *In Search Of Significance.*

We continued to receive gift cards and checks in the mail from people we knew and from people we had never heard of. When the new year arrived, we started looking more seriously for work. We had a little black IBM laptop computer and a printer and we put them to work on resumes and cover letters. Every morning we spent time together at breakfast, and during the day we did our best to network with other people and try to find work.

I believe God allows specific timing for things so we will know it is His will and that He is moving in our lives.

January came and went and so did February. The gift card and random checks in the mail manna stopped falling from heaven. March 1 Sherri and I finished the 60th and final entry in McGee's devotional book. Within the next two days, I was called by Tyler Media to sell advertising on their big country station and Sherri was contacted by a former work associate to manage the office of his new granite countertop company. Once again God shows up in a mighty way!

What a powerful and loving God we serve! He is rarely early, but He is never too late to take care of His children. He is the Good Shepherd who loves and cares for His lambs.

This past week I heard a podcast sermon from North Point Community Church in Atlanta, Georgia. The title of the sermon was "Promises." It was based on the 23rd Psalm. Read...

Psalm 23
A psalm of David.
[1] The LORD is my shepherd, I lack nothing.
[2] He makes me lie down in green pastures,
he leads me beside quiet waters,
[3] he refreshes my soul.
He guides me along the right paths
  for his name's sake.
[4] Even though I walk
  through the darkest valley,
I will fear no evil,
  for you are with me;
your rod and your staff,
  they comfort me.
[5] You prepare a table before me
  in the presence of my enemies.

You anoint my head with oil;
  my cup overflows.
[6] Surely your goodness and love will follow me
  all the days of my life,
and I will dwell in the house of the LORD
  forever.

My words: *I lack nothing, He supplies my every need. He leads me to nourishment. He refreshes my mind and heart. He guides me to the right business meetings for His name's sake. Even when bill collectors and the utility company is calling, I will not fear, because my Shepherd is with me. He takes care of me even when I get myself in a bind. His grace, mercy, and love are my constant companions. I will live with Him in His heavenly palace forever.*

The North Point preacher was pointing out all the specifics, sort of like I did earlier for my life, but then he stopped and said we have an action step to take if we want all of these great benefits. It's in the very first verse. "Action step?" I missed it. The action step is acknowledging the Lord is your Shepherd. You really can lean into Him and trust Him, if you have made it clear in your heart and in public that He IS your Shepherd.

The two main points I want to get across here…

1. You can trust God, no matter how bad your circumstances look.
2. ATAT (Accumulated Time Alone Together) can and will help you in your relationship with your wife.

You may be in a situation right now that seems overwhelming and out of your control. The fact is, it probably is overwhelming and out of your control. The good news for you today is if you have made the Lord your Shepherd, He is in control. It is not overwhelming for Him and it is not out of His control.

I like to encourage people. In the past I used to support my friends and work associates by saying "You have what it takes!" I no longer do that, because I found myself telling people that, who really didn't/don't have what it takes. Not because they are weak or stupid. I just don't want to encourage my brothers and sisters in Christ to trust in their own abilities. The sooner you realize your need to depend on God in all areas of your life, the better. Most of us will have a list of things we turn over to God and a list of things we can handle on our own.

You don't have what it takes, but your Shepherd does.

Chapter 10

PRIORITY NUMBER THREE

1. GOD 2. FAMILY 3. **JOB** 4. MINISTRY
5. RECREATION.

If you took your priority cues from TV and the world, your career or means of making money would clearly be your first priority in life. I like to watch Deadliest Catch on the Discovery Channel. Arguably one of the toughest jobs in the world today is working in the Baring Sea on a crab-fishing boat. The one thing we know for sure about these guys is they pretty much all have a terrible family life. They are gone out to sea for several months of the year. Many of the crew members work on other types of fishing vessels the rest of the year. With the use of satellite phones they can talk to family members every now and then. Most of the time, however, they are absent; leaving mom and kids back home in Alaska. They are praying their husband and father won't die at sea and that he will earn money while he is gone.

"Are you willing to give up your career for your wife and children?"

When you watch police/detective/crime drama type shows it's clear that the job always comes first. The main star is finally home with his family and the cell phone rings. He has to leave his family in the middle of dinner and deal with crime.

This is a real challenge for professionals who have gone to college and graduate school for 6 to 12 years and are now in their career. They have made such a huge investment into it, that it is difficult to *not* make it the hub of their lives. When your family becomes one of the spokes, it doesn't take long for problems to arise.

Whether you are a business owner, a dentist, or the president of the United States of America, at the end of your life, it was just a job for you to earn money to support your family. If you sacrifice your family for your career, you WILL regret it. No man lies on his deathbed and wishes he had put more time in at the office. When he lies alone, he only has regrets of the way he treated his wife, parents, and children.

In the early 1900's a pro baseball player received Christ as his savior and became an evangelist. His name was Billy Sunday. He has been credited with leading over 1 million people to Christ. That is wonderful, but he did this at the expense of his wife and children. At the end of his life, he was estranged from his wife and the famous evangelist's three sons died before he did of alcoholism and suicide.

The reason your job or career is your third priority, is because it is the tool God has given you to take care of your number two priority. Your job as daddy is not to take care of the world and save the world. Your job is to take care of your wife and children and make sure they are saved. What good would it be for a man to gain the whole world and lose his soul? There is something worse than that in my opinion. What good would it be for a man to save the entire world from sin and lose his own children? I speak as a preacher and missionary's kid who was blessed to have a father who made it clear we were more important to him than his work. He proved it to me one time as a freshman in high school when he missed an Elders meeting at the church to attend one of my football games. He communicated to them and to me where his priorities were, even though I barely got to play in those days.

ARE YOU WILLING TO GIVE UP YOUR CAREER/JOB FOR YOUR WIFE AND CHILDREN?

Your Career is just a Job.

Do your job as though unto the Lord. No matter what you do for a living, get up every day and do it as though He was your boss and you were working for Him. Take pride in whatever it is you do. Be excellent at whatever you put your hand to. No matter who your boss is or how mean or stupid he or she is, have a great attitude and know your Father up above is looking down with love.

Know also, *He is your provider and sustainer*.

If you lose your job doing what is right, it's okay. He will provide you with another opportunity to provide for your family.

When I was 13 years old I asked my father what a labor union was. He explained the best he could. He told me it was when workers of a big company join together and tell the owners and managers they will not work unless they get certain pay and benefit demands. That's pretty close. My reaction as a young teen was negative toward this. I said, "Wait a minute. All of the employees went to work for an agreed on salary or pay and then later they get together with other employees and blackmail the owners and managers into paying them more money? This doesn't sound right. Dad, where does trusting God for your daily needs fall under this?"

Whether trusting your union rep to make sure you are getting "what you deserve, " trusting your customers to pay their bills, or trusting your employer to pay you what and when he is supposed to pay you, you are placing your trust in the wrong person. Our God is our sustainer and provider! It all comes from him. Again, you are to do your work as though unto the Lord. Do your best every day. Arrive early, stay late, and leave your best while you are there. Trust God when you are hired and when you are fired.

I believe this is why tithing is important. When you tithe you are physically telling God you trust Him to take care of you. But, more about this later.

In the USA, you can be rich in a matter of seconds. All you have to do is recognize that you already are rich compared to the rest of the world. Wealth around the world is judged on whether you have running water or not. It's not if you own a home, but if you have running water where you live. If you have a car, you are in the top 2% of wealthy people in the world.

If you can read this book, you are rich compared to the rest of the world.

Your wife and family don't need you to earn more than your neighbors; they need you to pay your family's way. They need your example in trusting God every day. Your kids need to catch you praying and leaning into God for your needs.

IF POSSIBLE, YOU NEED TO GIVE YOUR WIFE THE MOST IMPORTANT JOB IN THE WORLD.

It's worth it for you to work extra hard for her to stay home with the kids when they are little. I know this won't work for everyone, but, in most cases, it's something you can plan ahead if you so choose.

S.A.H.M. ---Stay At Home Mom requires a sacrifice, it requires a lower standard of living. In our culture, in many cases it is easier to pay someone else to raise your kids. It is worth the sacrifice to drive old cars and live in old neighborhoods. You most likely grew up just a notch above the poverty line. For some reason when you were a kid, you never knew you were poor. That is, unless you lived near people who seemed wealthy.

The other option is:

D.I.N.K. ---Double Income No Kids. DINKS can plan ahead and choose having BMWs over having babies. There is nothing wrong with that. You and your wife can both work hard, buy cars and pay off your home and then have children.

Keep in mind if you are married, your second priority is your wife and your third is your job. Make sure you are spending the right amount of time with her, her parents, your siblings, and hers. This investment will pay off down the road when you need family members to assist you when "life" starts happening.

People get divorced over three things , Money, Kids and Sex. It's not over a lot of money, it's over enough money.

TITHE---MAKE GOD YOUR FINANCIAL PARTNER AND NEVER DEPEND ON YOUR CAREER OR JOB FOR YOUR PROVISION.

Chapter 11

PRIORITY NUMBER FOUR

1. GOD 2. FAMILY 3. JOB 4. **MINISTRY** 5. RECREATION.

Dr. Talley put it this way, "God gives us coupons of comfort through His word, through His Spirit and/or through His people. We are to pass them to others in acts of ministry, paying it forward."

This is where most pastors and ministry leaders get messed up. They usually get *God, Job,* and *Ministry* all combined as one big top priority and leave family and recreation behind. Your family needs to see and believe that they are more important than your job, your ministry, or your recreation.

My father was the Senior Pastor of a church with several hundred members. I was active in music and sports and often had practices Sunday nights and Wednesday nights. During football season we watched game films from the previous Friday night. I missed youth meetings and all types of church events. My father respected the choices I was making with my time and put no

"God really can turn your misery into your ministry!"

pressure on me "because he was the pastor." One Thursday night a church board meeting was scheduled the same time as one of my football games. My dad let them do the board meeting without him. He was at my game! He made it clear to me that night I was more important to him than his job and ministry.

Do your wife and kids know, without a doubt, they are more important than your career? It is just a job! It is simply your method for buying food and shelter. You may have an important job. You may be a federal court judge or a heart surgeon. Your wife and kids only see your career as "what you do to pay the bills." It is the most significant thing about your career.

Before you dive into any ministry I would like for you to meditate on 1 Corinthians 13:3. *"[3] If I give all I possess to the poor and give over my body to hardship that I may boast,[b] but do not have love, I gain nothing."*

Ministry is about love. Love is 1 Corinthians 13:4-8a. *"[4] Love is patient, love is kind. It does not envy, it does not boast, it is not proud. [5] It does not dishonor others, it is not self-seeking, it is not easily angered, it keeps no record of wrongs. [6] Love does not delight in evil but rejoices with the truth. [7] It always protects, always trusts, always hopes, always perseveres. [8]Love never fails."*

When you serve other people, they often don't have the capacity to fully appreciate and be grateful for what you are doing for them. If you are not serving from pure motives and love, you will become discouraged very quickly. It reminds me of a time I was in the 6th grade and a stray cat got stuck in our basement window. My father opened the window from the basement and gently reached in with his large hands. Even though my father was trying to help free the feline prisoner, it buried it's front claws into the top of his hands and began hissing like crazy. I had never seen a cat behave so angrily. After Dad was released from the claws, he went and got his big leather gloves and we were able to release the captive.

There will be times you pour yourself into someone else or an entire church and receive a black eye for your efforts. You simply have to "Work as though unto the Lord." Remain focused on the One Who served you by dying for you.

In the late 90's I was the pastor of a small church in rural Oklahoma. Our average attendance on Sundays was about 100. Easter Sunday is always big at every church. Many people only attend church on Christmas and Easter. My wife volunteered as our worship pastor, pianist, and choir director. This particular Easter, Sherri worked very hard putting together a praise team, band, and an amazing worship service. She even talked a guy named Mike Barnes into getting his drum set out of storage, dusting them off and giving our service a beat it had never heard before. Turned out Mike had been country music super-star Toby Keith's drummer a few years back and he was very good. The worship team practiced twice the week before Easter. I am sure Sherri put 30 hours into that Sunday's service. We ended up having two services and over 220 people in attendance (double our average). Later that day we had a small event at the church and then a few people stayed late to clean up. Sherri was exhausted and as we were walking to the car, a lady in the church walked up to her in the parking lot and began berating her for the horrible service that morning. She went on to say her son *finally* came to church and that he hated the drums. He said the drums ruined his experience. The lady basically blamed Sherri, if her son never came to church again. Needless to say, Sherri was crushed. It took her several weeks to recover from this punch to the gut.

I spent the first 12 years of my working career in paid ministry. I say paid, because I grew up a missionary's kid and a preacher's kid. I attended a Bible college and have been involved in ministry in one way or another for my entire life. In my opinion, ministry is serving other people in the name and through the power of Jesus Christ. Your service might be in feeding and clothing them. It might be teaching them a trade or skill to help them make a living. God made you with specific talents and gifts for serving Him, by serving others.

Jack Duvall Ministries

Over a half century ago a family named Duvall had a ministry. It was a simple one and they were consistent. Jack and Ruby Duvall picked up four extra children on their way to church every Sunday morning in rural north-east Oklahoma. They made it a priority to pick up the Jones kids every Sunday. Mary, Gene, Edna and Linda were able to attend Sunday School and Church every week at the Christian Church in Welch, Oklahoma. These four farm kids were able to learn of the saving grace of Jesus Christ due to the ministry of the Duvall family. Why do I care so much about their little weekly ministry? My mother was little Mary Jones. She grew up in that little church, chose Jesus as her Lord and Savior, and met her husband a few years later at church camp. My mother and father have influenced thousands of people for Christ as missionaries in Germany and in the ministry here in the United States. More importantly, my parents raised four Christian children who are all married, raising Christ followers themselves.

Coupons of Comfort

Your ministry might be one that comes straight from your scars. Many ministries begin on the backside of a mountain of pain. Every person who shows up at an Alcoholics Anonymous meeting is encouraged to go into ministry at their second meeting, or soon after. Part of the process of staying sober is becoming a sponsor for someone who has been sober for a shorter time than you.

As part of God's grace we were given coupons of comfort through His people, through His spirit and/or through His Word. Ministry is taking those "coupons" and passing them forward to other people who are hurting. God has a special way of preparing ministers for future hurting people.

A few months ago in my small group from church, we were talking about the verses at the beginning of the book of James. "Consider it pure joy, my brothers and sisters, whenever you face trials of many kinds, because you know that the testing of your faith produces perseverance. Let perseverance finish its work so that you may be mature and complete, not lacking anything." We were in a small circle of 6 or 8 people. I read the verse and when I looked up, a sweet lady named Anna had streams of tears running down her cheeks. I asked her if she was okay and she reassured me her tears were of joy.

Anna told our group that the "Consider it all joy…" verse used to be her least favorite in the Bible. She was severely abused as a child by a family member and every time she read that verse she had memories of her abuse. "How could I ever consider all of that pain joy???" Today she has a clear understanding and a heart of joy. Anna has four kids and is married to a pastor. Our church has a huge Celebrate Recovery ministry. She has had the opportunity to minister to many young victims of abuse giving them her coupons of comfort and a hope for the future. Through streaks of tears and a huge smile emerged, "I consider my abuse all joy for the sake of Christ in the lives of these ladies who show up at our church!"

You most likely have some scars making you eligible for ministry on a personal level.

God really can turn your misery into your ministry!

Chapter 12

Priority Number Five

1. GOD 2. FAMILY 3. JOB 4. MINISTRY
5. **RECREATION**.

Well you know what they say: "All work and no play makes Jack a dull boy." In addition to helping you lead a more interesting life, recreation is important because of the many health, social, and educational benefits it can provide. Even the word itself – recreation indicates that something in us is lost through our daily grind that needs to be replenished. We need to be re-created periodically, replenished, and built back up after a time of hard work.

If you watch a classroom full of third graders for a day, it should be fairly obvious why recreation is important. By the end of the day they look like they're about to jump out of their skin. They literally need to go outside and run around.

Adults are the same way; we're just better at hiding it because most of us aren't allowed an

"We need to be re-created periodically, replenished, and built back up after a time of hard work."

87

hour each day to play. We are expected to work, take care of our homes and families, and do responsible grown-up things. But if you take the time regularly to relax and enjoy yourself, you already know why recreation is important. Just in case you don't, however, here are just a few of the benefits of recreation:

- **Exercise** – If you play sports, dance, hike, walk or jog for fun, then you are not only refreshing your mind, but you are also helping your body to stay healthy and strong. Studies have shown that regular exercise can help prevent diseases, control your weight, increase strength, improve stamina, help you sleep better, and just make you feel better in general.
- **Fun and entertainment** – Some people will tell you that watching TV is a waste of time, or that it kills your brain cells. But, you know what? Sometimes your brain cells just need a rest, and if it makes you laugh, it's reducing stress and creating a more positive environment, especially if the laughs are shared with other people.
- **Relaxation** – This is hard for some people, but relaxation is necessary for good health. Our bodies aren't made to go non-stop all the time. We need sleep to regenerate, but we also need to consciously stop running around and sometimes just sit. Let the house get extra dusty one week, and read a good book instead of cleaning. Take your kids to the park, and let them play with other kids while you sit on a bench and soak up

the sun. Lie in bed for 10 minutes after you wake up in the morning, and just listen to the birds outside. Calm your mind, and you'll lower your blood pressure.

- **Group participation** – Participating in any kind of group activity – a class, theatrical production, community league sport, or pick-up game – has all kinds of benefits. Group activities help children build their social skills and help adults build their social networks. These social connections can later help the entire community because once people know each other, they are more likely to help each other and work together to make their neighborhoods better places to live.

- **Fresh air** – We can all agree that air-conditioning in the summer is a good thing, but by sitting inside all the time, you're breathing in all kinds of disgusting stuff, from tiny pieces of cockroaches and spiders to byproducts of your family members' or coworkers' flatulence. Get outside, even if it's just to sit for 15 minutes in the sun. The sun's vitamin D will do you good too.

Defining Recreation

Recreation is any mental or physical refreshment achieved by way of play (games, sports, or hobbies), amusement, or relaxation. Recreation can take many various forms and everyone enjoys different recreational activities.

The ways that people refresh themselves are literally countless. You can do anything from building model airplanes to jumping out of real airplanes. You can:
- Read a book or magazine
- Watch a movie or YouTube videos
- Watch clouds
- Play a musical instrument
- Play ultimate Frisbee
- Go hiking
- Go swimming
- Lie on the couch
- Lie in a field
- Walk on the beach
- Walk around downtown
- Bake cookies

Whatever gets you out of your normal work life and into some sort of amusement can be considered recreation.

Recreation is important for your physical and mental health. Give it a try for a month and see how you feel. And if you're still not on board, just remember that in the Biblical story of creation, even God rested.

Chapter 13

Financial Leadership

When a couple is in the middle of a divorce, rest assured that money problems were a key factor in their split. Money problems can present themselves in a variety of ways. The pursuit of more and not being content with what we have can put us on a course we don't want to be on later in life.

The irony of this is that separation and divorce always cause more financial pain than there was in the marriage and the divorce process will not make you a better steward of your money.

From the time we get married we set goals for ourselves regarding the amount of money we make, the size and quality of our home, vacations, cars, and more. The problem with most of these is they are moving targets. What you considered a financial goal when you were first married, will not seem to be enough after you have kids. Another challenge we have in America is peer pressure and living in a materialistic society

"Separation and divorce always cause more financial pain than there was in the marriage."

that teaches us we will be happy if we have more of everything. We are never allowed to be content with what we have, because happiness is… a little bit more and a little bit better quality.

There is nothing wrong with striving for success financially as long as you have your priorities in order at home. The mistake we men make is making money assumptions about our wives. We assume our lady wants more and better more than anything else in life. In most cases our marital dialog is about more and better.

Listen to me here… THE MAIN THING YOUR WIFE NEEDS IS FINANCIAL SECURITY, NOT A BETTER HOUSE, FURNITURE AND OTHER STUFF. She may spend time every day talking about the stuff she wishes she had, but the foundation of her security rests on knowing your family has enough to pay your way every month.

As the financial leader in your home, you will have to *be willing to give up short term approval, for long-term respect.*

Joe and Gladys Grimaud have been friends of mine for many years. One of my favorite stories Gladys tells regarding this, happened over 50 years ago. When they were in their first few years of marriage Joe was a young enlisted man in the Air Force and they lived in Topeka, Kansas. One day they were at a non-air-conditioned Laundromat in mid-July, during the heat of the day. While washing their clothes, Gladys had a sudden desire for an ice cream cone. Now, in those days you could get an ice cream cone for a nickel. Gladys said, "Joe, I want an ice-cream cone." Joe said, "Gladys, we don't have the money to spend on ice cream." Gladys felt hurt and began to cry. Joe embraced her and said, "Honey, someday I will buy you all the ice-cream you can eat, but today we just can't afford it." Joe's military take home pay was $191.00 a month. The first $19.10 went to the church they attended. That left $171.90 for them to live on. They had a budget written on ruled notebook paper taped to the wall right by the door of their little one bedroom house trailer, and it listed $30 a month for food. They survived by living within that budget. Their diet consisted of dried peas and beans and hamburger meat about once a week. Joe knew if they spent any money on things like ice-cream, they would go hungry at the end of the month. Today Joe and Gladys are wealthy business owners who are able to give tons of money to hurting people and ministries all over the world.

Tithing

I mentioned tithing as a great tool for you regarding your job in an earlier chapter. "Give God your first and your best and He will take care of the rest." When you are partnering with God in your finances, you look to Him for your provision, and not your job. Jobs come and go, but God is your consistent provider!

Tithing is what Joe and Gladys did and still do. If you and your wife are Christ followers, it would be a good idea for you to participate in tithing together. This just means that you give the first 10% of your money back to God through the local church. By returning the first 10% of your income to God, you are making a statement to God and to yourself that you trust Him to take care of all your needs. This is a principle that you can put to the test. As a matter of fact the Bible encourages us to test God in this area. *Bring the whole tithe into the storehouse, that there may be food in my house. Test me in this," says the LORD Almighty, "and see if I will not throw open the floodgates of heaven and pour out so much blessing that you will not have room enough for it.* (Malachi 3:10)

About ten years ago, the pastor of our church was preaching on this principle. He and the church leadership team decided to take this to a new level and announced publically the church would help you test God on this. If anyone in the church would tithe for 90 days and God did NOT show up and prove Himself during that time, our church would give that individual a check back for the entire amount they tithed. Many, many people have taken the challenge and to my knowledge our Creator has come through for his people every time. By tithing, you are taking God's hand financially and involving him in your daily journey providing for your family.

If you are a new Christian, or if you have not trusted God in this area of your life, now is a good time to begin.

The challenges we face as Americans is the lifestyle we lead. Many, if not most of us, are living on more than we earn or at least we are not saving any money. Logic would tell us that we can't take a 10% piece out of the pie and still make it financially every month. This is not a logic exercise; this is a trusting God-faith exercise.

Tithing is making God your partner in all things financial. You give God your first and best, and He will take care of the rest!

What does this have to do with your relationship with your wife? This demonstrates both financial and spiritual leadership on your part for her. Two of the three areas she needs to be secure in are financial and spiritual.

If you are working to improve your relationship with your wife, visit with her about this quite a bit before you begin. Most likely she will respect your efforts to do God's will in this area of your life.

Dr. Talley has a great system for beginners regarding tithing. Since your faith is small in this area, when you begin you should start small and allow your faith to grow into the tithe and then into giving offerings above that. His system in simple, you work up to the tithe one month at a time for 10 months. The first month you return to God 1%, then 2% the next month, 3% the third month and so on until you reach 10%.

In Dr. Talley's experience, he has seen many people tithe 10% the first month. It was difficult for them, so in the second month they held on to their tithe money for the first two weeks and then gave it. The third month would never make it to the offering plate. His suggestion is that your faith-muscle is weak in the beginning, so you should start with a smaller "weight." It's hard to give up 10% when you have no, or 1% faith. Take this faith journey with your wife, one month at a time. Spend time with her in prayer over this. Ask God to show Himself to you in your finances.

In most cases, the tithe will come easier for your wife than it will for you. Things of the spiritual nature and trusting God seem to be more intuitive and easier to grasp for women than for men. You are also making a commitment together that you trust God for your daily needs. Tithing together will help her look past you and toward God for her needs. Over time, as you both see God show up in your financial lives, her faith and yours will grow to a point of peace in finances.

Let's make something clear: I did not say if you tithe God will make you wealthy. I am saying he will give you peace in the area of money. For some reason money flows toward some Christians and others can't seem to hold on to any of it. The point is to become like the apostle Paul as he writes in Philippians 4:10-12

[10] I rejoiced greatly in the Lord that at last you renewed your concern for me. Indeed, you were concerned, but you had no opportunity to show it. [11] I am not saying this because I am in need, for I have learned to be content whatever the circumstances. [12] I know what it is to be in need, and I know what it is to have plenty. I have learned the secret of being content in any and every situation, whether well fed or hungry, whether living in plenty or in want.

No matter what our financial situation is, we need to reach a point where we are content and we rejoice in our circumstances, no matter what they are.

You may be a person who has been very disciplined with money and you have been able to save a lot and buy nice things. We still live in a world where bad things happen to well-disciplined people. Your nest-egg can disappear overnight.

When hurricane Katrina hit New Orleans, there were many solid, Christian, disciplined people who lost their home and were wiped out financially. It's not so devastating when you have been walking with God financially and you know He will take care of you.

Do you know of, or have you ever heard of a Christian community, village, or nation that starved to death? Throughout Christian history, it has always been Christ-following people who bring food, water and the Gospel to starving pagans of the world.

Lean into God financially and you can have financial peace. (Thank you, Dave Ramsey, for helping so many people!)

FINANCIAL PEACE

The Lord has truly blessed our country with Dave Ramsey. One great way for you and your wife to get on the same page regarding finances is to sign up for Financial Peace University at a church somewhere. If you can't find a church group leading this class, contact the people at www.DaveRamsey.com and lead a group yourself. It's pretty simple; you watch videos and fill out some workbooks. He teaches how to get out of debt and build wealth the way your grandparents did, the way God recommends it in the Bible.

The main thing you learn are Dave's baby steps:

1. Make a decision not to get into any more debt.
2. Start with a $1000.00 emergency fund.
3. Pay off debt using the "Debt Snowball." This is a system Dave Ramsey teaches to pay off debt starting with smallest, working up to largest.
4. Build your savings account up to 3 to 6 months of your income.
5. Invest 15% of household income into Roth IRAs and pre-tax retirement savings.
6. College funding for your children, (If needed).
7. Pay home off early.
8. Continue to build wealth and GIVE. (Money is a tool; use it to help people and expand the Kingdom of God.)

This is my summary of Ramsey's baby steps. You can find out much more online.

Chapter 14

Just Enough

YOU DON'T HAVE TO HAVE A LOT, JUST
ENOUGH TO PAY YOUR WAY.

In 2005 I quit working for a company where I was
earning a descent amount of money. While working
there, I moved my family of seven into a large house
where we were paying $2500 a month for housing,
including utilities. In the fall, when I quit, I started my
own business with a yellow legal pad, a broken laptop
computer and $200. I worked very hard to get my
income to a point where we could afford to live in that
house, but struggled. I made a tough call that my wife
did not like. I moved our family into an apartment,
cutting our housing costs in half. In business, this is
called **cutting your overhead**. Business leaders know
in order to remain profitable and stay in business, you
sometimes have to let some
employees go and sell some
assets. For some reason
many family leaders think
the answer is to go into
debt in order to make ends
meet. Because we moved
into a smaller place we
were able to sell a lot of
furniture and stuff we

> *"You have to be
> willing to give
> up short term
> approval, for
> long term
> respect."*

didn't need. Business leaders often **sell assets** in order to have cash flow to keep the business running. For some reason family leaders put their stuff in a storage unit and go into debt with second mortgages and credit cards.

The other thing I had to do was **increase my income**. My wife and I have always agreed she would be home with our kids at least until they are all in school. This meant it was up to me to figure out ways to increase our income while at the same time growing my own business. At one time I took on a job throwing newspapers seven days a week. I developed a good relationship with my landlord and he started giving me handy-man jobs. During that time I painted rental houses, I built privacy fences, and did all kinds of yard work. I also worked weekends cooking in a commercial kitchen. This has been a valuable lesson for my kids. They know how important it is to do whatever it takes. Sometimes whatever it takes is not fun at all, but necessary.

There were times I was concerned about what other people might think of me. I have a marketing and advertising company and was concerned about what my clients might think, or what potential clients might think. That's where you go back to… "You have to be willing to give up short term approval, for long term respect".

A few years back I worked with a lady whose husband lost his job as an engineer. He was making good money and then ended up drawing unemployment for a while. He would not consider taking any job, except for the one he was trained to do. This put a tremendous burden on his wife to make even more money at her job. He continued to apply places and get his resume in front of people, but would not take any other job. Over time the financial stress got the best of her and she kicked him out. They are now divorced. He refused to humble himself and show his wife how much he loves her and their kids by doing whatever it takes to support them.

After six months in the apartment, we definitely needed more square footage, so we moved financially horizontal into an old, dusty, creaky house with pink ugly siding. My wife hated the house and let me know about once a month. She did like the fact that we were not getting shut off notices and the debt collectors stopped calling. We stayed in that house for two years and then found a nicer, newer, more energy efficient rental home that made another horizontal move financially. We may have been paying a little bit more a month overall, but it was worth it regarding my wife's feelings about her "nest." The old house never felt clean enough for her, so she was never at peace regarding how clean it was. The newer place made her feel better about her life, family and home. That's worth some money!

Chapter 15

Get a Suzie

My marriage hit a three-year rough spot from 2000 to 2003. During that time we didn't trust each other and needed help making financial decisions together for our family. I was telling a friend, Allison, at work about some of the issues my wife and I were dealing with. Allison said I needed to go to Suzie for help. "Who is Suzie?" Suzie started her own business years ago as a bookkeeper for businesses, but also helped families as a bookkeeper. Allison grew up in a family where she learned nothing about money management and for the past 10 years Suzie and her company helped Allison and her husband, Bob, stay on top of all things financial. On her referral, my wife Sherri and I hired Suzie to help us. Over a few meetings Suzie and her staff got to know us and our financial goals. She helped us put them into writing and made a plan for us to follow. In the beginning we met with her every Thursday during our lunch break. Suzie helped us keep our checkbook balanced and kept us on a budget

"No matter the issue, you either have to discipline yourself to do it yourself or hire someone to do it for you."

paying our bills and giving us each gas, food, and spending money every week. We rarely if ever argued about money during that time, because we both knew to bring all things financial to Suzie and she would help us make the right decision that was in line with our plan. One time I spent some money that was not on our plan. I used my bank check card. At our next Suzie-meeting, she asked for the card, I gave it to her, she put it in her file and I stayed on track from then on.

I have talked to a few people over the years who were critical of hiring someone to help with money discipline.

They told me we should learn be more disciplined. Using the same logic, I told them they should no longer hire someone to help them with their taxes. If they were truly disciplined, they would learn all the tax codes and file their own taxes with no help. I could go on and on about changing your own oil, mowing your own lawn, cleaning your house, or whatever you hire other people to do in your world. The fact is, we were, and many times are, weak at disciplining ourselves with money and we need help in that area.

No matter the issue, you either have to discipline yourself to do it yourself or hire someone to do it for you.

Chapter 16

Better Sex

About two months into writing this book, it happened the first time. I did and said something pretty stupid to my wife. I don't remember what it was, but she said, "Why don't you take your own advice from the book you are writing…!?" Ouch! I didn't do any writing for a week after that.

Who do I think I am writing this book to help men with their most important earthly relationship. I apologized and fixed whatever it was I did wrong and Sherri let me know I should not give up on this project. Every book ever written was written by messed up people. The Bible was written by adulterers, liars, and murderers. I will keep plugging away on this project with Dr. Talley.

The topic of sex makes me a bit nervous to talk about. It is difficult enough to talk about with my wife of 25 years. I don't want people to think I am an expert in this area; far from it. I have had good moments and terrible moments in this area. Maybe I will learn something that I

"Men are like fighter jets, we can take off at a moment's notice with little fuel or runway."

can apply to my own life in the process of writing this.

My main goal is to remind you of the difference between you and your wife. I also want to point out the things you have in common.

The most encouraging thing I picked up about a year ago from my friend Paul Iser. He asked me how I did overall when it comes to handling arguments and intimacy issues. I said on a scale of 1 to 10, I was about a 4. He said, "Wow, you are batting 400!!! If you were a major league baseball player, you would be one of highest paid and most famous players in the country!"

That was about as encouraging a thing I had ever heard. I have always known nobody is perfect, but no one is even near perfect. When it comes to relationships, we men are as far from perfect as we can get.

The Basics

Let's go over the basic differences you may have heard before.

For her sex begins at breakfast, maybe even breakfast the day before your date night. For you sex begins two seconds after you think about it.

You are more likely to become turned on by, well… pretty much anything! Mainly, it has to do with what you are seeing and thinking about. You can be in the same room with your wife, look at her and be ready for sex in 60 seconds. You don't need any more time than that. You don't need to talk to her, snuggle with her, or get warmed up in any way. She is different. You may not want to believe it, but it's true. There may be times in your sexual history with her that she was ready pretty fast, but most likely she was thinking about it many hours before the event.

Dr. Talley puts it this way for us men to understand better. Men are like fighter jets, we can take off at a moment's notice with little fuel or runway. We can't fly very far and we can only shoot one missile before we have to take a refuel and reload break. As men get older, they are happy when they can shoot any missile at all. Your wife is more like a bomber. She requires a lot more time to get ready for take-off. She might need to start fueling up and loading the bombs the day before the mission.

Your jet has one engine and one person in the cockpit. You are only thinking about one thing when you fire it up.

She is multi-tasking about everything, all the time. She has at least four engines. For them to all run smoothly, her world must be in order. Are the kids in bed and asleep? Did I turn on the dishwasher? Did I turn off the oven? Did the trash go out? Does little Johnny have what he needs for school in the morning? Is the door locked? How am I doing physically? Did I just end my period? Is it about to start? Did I take a bath with my favorite soaps and oils? Are the candles lit? Has my husband showed me he cares about me? Has he been sweet to me? Have we communicated well with each other the past few days? Did he say something stupid that hurt my feelings today?

When you have done your part for her and she is ready, her bomber mission can keep going long after you have fired your missile. She also can carry many bombs that can explode one after another.

CONSISTENCY ALWAYS OUTPERFORMS OCCASIONAL BRILLIANCE!

Years ago when my wife and I were going to see Dr. Talley for marriage help, naturally the topic of sex came up. I would rather have my fingernails pulled out with rusty needle-nose pliers than talk about my sex life with my wife and a counselor.

To start the dialog, he gave us each a yellow post-it note and asked us to write down how often we have sex, how often we would like to have sex and how often we think our spouse wants to have sex. I wrote down once a month, I would like to have sex at least once a week, and I think she wants to have sex twice a year. (I wasn't kidding.) She wrote we have sex twice a month, for her once a week would be good, and she thought I wanted to have sex every day.

Doc read the notes and started laughing. "What we have here is a problem communicating. You both could live with and would like having sex

"One couple he counseled had gone for over two years without sex, because of a conflict they were having over one of their children."

once a week."

He went on to say he believes that should be the goal for every married couple and that it is not only important for your emotional relationship, it is also important for each of us physiologically. We both need the release it gives in lowering tension and stresses of life.

For some reason we ended up agreeing on having a date night every Tuesday night. That may sound un-romantic and too predictable for you, but it helped us. It took pressure off of both of us. I no longer feared going long periods of time without sex and I didn't feel like I had to jump through the right hoops in order to get lucky with my wife. I made sure I was being sweet to her and it made it easier to mention on Monday. We would start talking about our date night the day before and that made it better for both of us.

Some weeks there is more and some weeks none at all, but overall we try to be consistent.

Dr. Talley told us about many couples that don't have sex if they are in an argument or disagreement about something. One couple he counseled had gone for over two years without sex, because of a conflict they were having over one of their children. He told them to put their argument aside, have their sex and then pick it back up the next day. *(This does not apply if you have done something to hurt your wife's feelings.)*

Change Your Expectations

Stop talking to your buddies about their sex life, they are lying!

An acquaintance of mine would mention every now and then that he and his wife have a great sex life. He would say they do it at least three times a week. (I didn't want to know and I wonder about a guy who feels the need to talk about such things.) Then at other times he would complain about how long it has been for him, because of family and job issues. Most likely he was lying about the former.

Do yourself a favor and do not listen to anything other men have to say about their sex life. In most cases they are stretching the truth or all out lying.

Talking to my wife, I mentioned something I heard a friend of mine say about his love life and wife. Sherri simply said, "I didn't marry that guy, I married you. You didn't marry her, you married me."

Treat her like you treated her when she was your girlfriend.

Think back to when you were dating. Before you were married and you were still on "the hunt," you treated her differently than you do now. Why? Your expectations have changed. Before you were married you had no expectations. You were delighted with a kiss at the end of a date. She was mysterious and exciting. When you have no expectations of another person, whatever they do for you is very much appreciated. When you start expecting something, you no longer feel grateful for their actions.

When my wife and I were going to Dr. Talley for marriage help a few years back, one of the things he asked us to do was to lower our expectations of each other to zero. In every area of our relationship and life together, we were to expect nothing of each other. The very first thing I noticed after we had that conversation is what I called "The Magic Underwear Drawer." With my new mind set of NO expectations, I opened my underwear drawer one Sunday morning before church and realized it was full of clean white t-shirts and my white cotton briefs. I exclaimed, "Wow, this is a magic underwear drawer! Yesterday morning it was empty and this morning I open it and it is full of fresh, clean underwear!" I walked over to my wife, kissed her on the cheek and thanked her for all the laundry she did the day before. (Did I mention we have five kids?)

There is a line in one of my wife's favorite movies, *Pretty Woman,* starring Richard Gere and Julia Roberts. If you know the movie, the main man of the movie is a super-rich business man who needed a date for a big meeting. He was recently divorced and didn't want to get into a relationship, so he hired a prostitute to be his date. After she was paid well, he first had to train her in the right etiquette before he paraded her around at the meeting. When they were back in his hotel suite later, he was not acting interested in her sexually. She makes some statement along the lines of, "Hey, c'mon. I am a SURE THING."

You might be married, but you need to lower your expectations of your wife to zero and never count on her being a sure thing. Even if she tells you she is a sure thing, she still wants to be talked to and pursued by you as though she were not.

This business of zero expectations of each other is a wonderful thing. It's how friends treat each other. Think about it, when you get together with your best male friend for any reason, what are your expectations of him? You might have a small expectation of where and when you are going to meet, but after that you have none. On top of that, you are very grateful for anything they do for you.

In what areas to you have expectations of your bride? Cooking? Cleaning? Taking care of kids? Laundry? Sex?

Make a list of every single job and chore she does. Reset your mind right now. From now on you will have no expectations of her in any area of life. The next time she does one of them, thank her. The next time she drops the ball on one of them, step in and help her. Then thank her for the other things she does.

Chances are pretty good she will start lowering her expectations of you as well and that is a pretty sweet way to live together.

"He asked me if I knew about a certain food that kills sexual appetite..."

More tips for a better sex life...

When Doc and I first started talking about this topic, he asked me if I knew about a certain food that kills sexual appetite. I guessed, sugar, too many carbs... The entire time he was smiling and shaking his head no. He then said, "Wedding cake!" We both laughed for a minute. He went on to say when he is doing pre-marital counseling; he can't get them to keep their hands off of each other no matter what their age. "Forbidden fruit is just so much sweeter..." Then after they are married a few years, the novelty wears off for one or both of them.

In most cases the novelty wears off for her first.

Dr. Talley's quote: "You made the witch you live with!"

Chances are, before you were married and the first few years of your marriage you probably had a pretty good sex life. Then over time, she quit responding to you the way she did in the beginning.

They key word in the last sentence is "RESPONDING," Doc went on to say, "Women are responders. **If you don't like the way she is responding to you, change the way you initiate."**

He told me about a couple he counseled a few years back. They had been married for over twenty years. She started having an affair right after their last child went off to college. The husband was very angry and hurt sitting there in Doc's office. What kind of woman would go off and start having an affair after such a long marriage? It turns out, after they got married he got grouchy and mean. And after they got married she never had an orgasm with her husband. Never. Doc said: "You can't yell at her and call her names and expect her to have an orgasm!"

He went on to tell me she had one every time with her boyfriend. Neither were willing to make any changes in their lives, they divorced and she married her boyfriend.

Think back for a moment…

How did you treat her in every area of life, before you were married?

When you asked her out on a date and she said yes, you were happy, proud and grateful!

You could talk for hours on the phone about nothing.

You cared about your personal grooming.

You wore your best clothes.

You used the best language around her.

If you had to wait for her, you didn't mind.

You were polite to her parents and siblings.

"If you don't like the way she is responding to you, change the way you initiate."

You tolerated her friends.

You played cards and board games with her.

You never tried to control her.

You encouraged her and let her know how smart she was.

You encouraged her to dream and reach for the stars.

Her education was important to you.

You took her to dinner with no expectations thereafter.

You liked to take a walk with her holding hands.

You could sit on a porch swing with her for hours.

You played racquetball or some other sport with her.

When she wanted to talk, you could listen to every word for hours.

You were sensitive to her feminine needs and issues.

You cared about what she cared about.

You liked to eat what she liked to eat.

You did not belch or fart in her presence.

You cleaned up after yourself in her presence.

You cleaned out your car, vacuumed it and sprayed smelly stuff in it before a date.

Compare how you used to be, to now. Change is normal. I don't know anyone who hasn't changed in their relationship over time. If you don't like the way your wife responds to you sexually, it's time for you to initiate in a different way. Shock her out of her mind by making your next date night all about her. If you never have date nights, it's time to start. First, ask your wife if she would do you the pleasure of going on a date with you. If she responds confused or negatively, give her some time, wait a week and ask her again. You are engaging in a long-term process to demonstrate to her that you are a different person than you have been the past few years.

When you were dating, it was all about her. Make it all about her again; what she likes to do and where she likes to eat. After she tells you she would like to go out with you, you arrange for a babysitter. Ask the babysitter to come an hour or two early so your wife can get ready without any child-eruptions. If you can't do that, take the kids away from the house while she is getting ready and return them to the house when the babysitter shows up. Take her to a restaurant she enjoys and after dinner go on a walk with her someplace peaceful and relaxing. You might be married to a gal who loves to do what you like to do. For her a great date might be going fishing or paintball. Try to do something she knows you could care less about.

Remember, your goal is to make her feel like you did when you were dating. You know, special... like a princess. She wants to be pursued by her knight in shining armor.

Don't give up on her. You didn't get where you are today overnight. If you don't like the way she is responding to you, change the way you initiate.

More advice from Dr. Talley...

Do what it takes to help her become relaxed.

I mentioned earlier that ladies are much better at multi-tasking than we knuckle-draggers. It's great when it comes to managing the household, volunteering, and holding down a job. The down side is, when mom is at home, her brain rarely shuts down and relaxes. When she is home, there is always something that needs to be cleaned, read, signed, cooked, washed, folded, cut, repaired, or put away. If you have kids, your sex-life will or has been interrupted. When you have a baby, you are just hoping for one un-interrupted hour for a little bit of physical contact. After they are out of the crib, you can expect a knock at the door at the wrong time.

A friend of mine told me about a time he and his wife were in the throes of passion when they were interrupted by a three year old voice at the foot of their bed. "Ooooo, yuck, bottoms!" The few words took the temperature of the room down many degrees.

My wife and I have five kids. We have always been good at keeping the door locked, but have been interrupted multiple times and ways. Most recent was by a cell phone. Four of our five kids have cell phones. One night the older four were all spending the night other places and our five year old was fast asleep. I locked the front door and our bedroom door. Right as we were making some progress, my wife's phone rang. She glanced over to the night-stand and could see it was our 13 year old daughter. "I better get that, just in case we (you) need to go get her." She asked her mother a question or two and said good night. She turned her ringer off and her attention back toward me, then MY phone started vibrating on top of my dresser! I was going to turn my ringer off and accidentally hit the green button. Fortunately I heard my 17 year old son, "Dad, hey dad. I have a question for you about my car. For some reason the heater is not getting hot. What do you think the problem is?" My wife whispered, "Be nice..." I had a five minute conversation with my son about his car and that concluded our romance for the evening.

I said all of that to say this: If you can afford it, or if you are willing to afford it, have a date night that ends up at a hotel. When I am able to get my wife away from the house and all the issues thereof, she is able to enjoy herself much, much more. You might think it's too much money to spend on your date. Trust me, it's worth it. You will be amazed how affordable it can be with some of the websites like Priceline.com, Expedia, and other sites like that. We have paid as little as $40 for a nice room at a nice place. You can drop a hundred bucks on dinner and a movie pretty fast. Why not spend half the money on a room that will guarantee you no interruptions?

Dr. Talley says, "Practice safe sex!"

When she feels safe, the sex is better.

If there is any thought in her mind that she could get pregnant, it will affect her ability to relax and enjoy herself. (UNLESS YOU ARE TRYING TO HAVE A BABY.)

If you both know you have had all the kids you want, do something permanent about baby-making. Get a vasectomy. It will only affect you for a couple of days and when you are healed up, she will probably reward you for your sacrifice.

Don't try to get much sympathy from her though, she bore your children. No matter what you think, carrying your children and delivering them was a bigger deal than a ten minute out-patient procedure.

Dr. Talley says, "Never, never reject her!"

In the course of your marriage, your wife may say no to your sexual advances 100,000 times. If and when she initiates sex, never, never reject her. Her self-image and self-worth is more fragile than yours. How you treat her matters.

Doc says men are like beer steins, you know the big tough German beer mugs. Ladies are more like wine glasses or Champaign flutes. We men can say all kinds of tough things to each other regarding our body parts and our sex lives. When we men clank our big mugs against each other it might chip our paint or make a tiny crack, but there is no huge damage. We heal up pretty

119

fast in most cases. For some of us, it adds some character.

What do you think happens when your big beer stein clanks into your bride's delicate wine glass? It shatters. Putting it back together is very difficult.

Rejecting your sweet wife's advances will very likely do major damage to the possibility of your future advances in the same area.

Besides that, there are men all over the world that would love for their wife to initiate sex just one time before they die. If they found out about you, they might just track you down and kick your butt!

Chapter 17

Protect your marriage!

Love your marriage enough to protect it. Sex is better when she knows you are willing to do whatever it takes!

If there is anything from your past that might show up in your future, pull that skeleton out of the closet and throw it in the middle of the living room floor. It might be awkward when you do, but not as awkward as if it pops up later and it looks like you are trying to cover something up

Guess what? You don't expect the same from her. If she wants to share things from her past, she can. But this is about her trusting you, not you trusting her. That's for some other book. Total and continual transparency and honesty from you to her, nothing less. Pray and ask God to bring things to the forefront of your mind that you may have forgotten.

"Six months later they met in person and three months after that they started playing 'Naked City' together."

Facebook and the Internet...

Sadly, Dr. Talley counsels couples every week who are having major challenges due to the rekindling of old flames. Make sure your wife knows every username and password to any application you use on the Internet. Share an email account with her and keep no secrets ever.

Don't "friend" sexual partners from your past on Facebook or on any other social marketing application. Stay away from anything that has to do with dating or flirting on the Internet.

Use common sense when you are on your computer!

She wants to be confident you are monogamous. Do everything you can do to help her know that. I am not just talking about having sex with some other woman; I am talking about being intimate with your words as well. You can have an emotional affair that can be as damaging to your monogamy as a physical one. All sexual affairs started with emotional words.

Tim is a guy I am acquainted with. He is married, has two little daughters and has a girlfriend. His girlfriend was his girlfriend in high school. She has always liked him. Tim and his wife have had relational difficulties for several years. I always thought his wife was sort of a witch. Most likely she got that way over time and I am sure *he's* not all syrup and honey at home. About a year ago he "friended" his old girlfriend on Facebook and began an ongoing dialog with her. Six months later they met in person and three months after that they started playing "Naked City" together. (If you know what I mean…)

The world would say, "Go with your heart!" "Do what feels right!" The world would tell his wife to divorce him and get on with her life. Actually that's what she would hear from her Christian friends at church. Dr. Talley has often said the most damaging words church people often say to people in Tim's wife's position is GET ON WITH YOUR LIFE. They are saying you have the right and you deserve to abandon this marriage. You may have the right scripturally to leave your spouse, but that does not make it the best thing for you to do. You also have the right to smoke and drink, and but that may not be the best thing for you to do. The best thing for Tim and his wife is for Tim to cut off all communication with his girlfriend; then for Tim to sincerely beg forgiveness and then for his wife to forgive him. Then they both need to work on their relationship where they will learn to like and love each other again. That is the best thing for the husband, the wife and the kids!

Christian Businessmen Beware!

Psalms 37:12 says, "The wicked hunt for the soul of the righteous." If you are in the business world and you are a Christian,

"Take every precaution you can when you are out in the world to protect your marriage and family."

123

know in your knower that the enemy is out to steal, kill, and destroy. He does not want your family to succeed! He wants you to fail. He wants your family split up and his agents are busy at work.

My brother travels a lot for the company he works for. He is married to a beautiful lady and has a wonderful daughter. A few years back my brother told me about a situation that had recently happened. A very nice looking female sales rep that worked for a sister company ended up at a few of the same events as my brother. She took a liking to my brother and asked him if they could spend some time alone together. He was polite to her and let her know he was happily married. The next night at dinner she approached him again and once again he politely sent her packing. Later the same evening she approached him again, a little tipsy with a drink in her hand. She made another pass at him right there in front of everyone. My brother walked away and headed to his room to escape her talons. About thirty minutes later the phone in his room rang. It was she, again! This time he let her have it verbally and asked her to never speak to him again.

The next day a work colleague of my brother's told him that lady was known for trying to bed "righteous married men." Wow! I was naïve and had never heard of such evil. Psalms 37:12 says, "They band together against the righteous and condemn the innocent to death." I am talking about this to let you know to be on your guard at all times. If you play with fire, the prince of fire and darkness will help you burn yourself. The enemy's goal is not just for you to get burned, but to incinerate you and your family.

Take every precaution you can when you are out in the world to protect your marriage and family.

1. Don't eat dinner or lunch alone with any female other than your wife, daughter, mom or sister.
2. When you travel on business, do not travel alone. Do so with another man, not a woman.
3. Make sure the men you travel with know what you stand for and know to hold you accountable to your values.
4. Communicate often to your wife about what you are doing in detail.
5. Do not drink alcohol when you are out of town traveling. You become most vulnerable at that point. The part of your brain that makes good choices gets shut off. The enemy knows this and sends his people your way to tempt you and tear you down.

Make sure you ask your wife and other family members to be praying for you when you are traveling. I am convinced my kids, parents, and my in-laws were praying for me during the time my wife and I were having our biggest challenges. Sherri and I were somewhere in the second year of not getting along very well. We were invited to a business Christmas dinner party. Sherri didn't want to go. In fact she went to some other party with a friend of hers. I went to the big dinner party to represent the business I worked for. I sat at a table with a few people I knew. The ones I knew were at my left and a nice, very attractive lady about 10 years older than I was to my right with her husband. He was a pretty well known business owner in our city. I was my normal, friendly self and visited with the lady during dinner. Right before desert was served I got up to get myself some more to drink. This lady followed me. She walked over to the bar and got another glass of wine. It was sort of warm, so I walked over to the main entrance where a little bit of cool air was coming in. Before I knew it, the beautiful lady was standing in front of me with her glass of wine and her low-cut evening gown. She smiled and asked me if I wanted to go out and check out her new car with her. Because of my lack of experience and my naiveté, I thought she really wanted to show me her new car. Without a thought, words started coming out of my mouth. I said, "I can't, I really need to be getting home right now. I have four kids at home and their mother won't be home till late and they have school tomorrow." I walked straight to my car and went home.

About five miles down the road, what just happened finally occurred to me. Tears filled my eyes at that point. I pulled my car off the road and put it in park. I believe the prayers of my family were answered miraculously that night. I believe the Holy Spirit took total control of my mind and body for a short period of time to protect me from a Psalms 37:12 woman.

If you go out looking for trouble, trouble will find you!

Chapter 18

Her Security

As we travel through life, you find out more and more differences between men and women. You may have heard someone say the primary need of women is security and the primary need for men is significance. I asked Dr. Talley to elaborate on this one morning over breakfast. I thought he was going to give me an illustration or some nugget of truth to back up these observations about the sexes. It turns out he told me there are five legs of a woman's security needs. (We men have our needs also, but that's for another book when we are concerned with your needs.) They are physical, emotional, relational, spiritual, and financial.

Physical Security

We men don't spend a lot of time thinking about our physical safety and security unless we happen to be hanging out in a bad neighborhood. As a rule, we don't think about being a victim of some kind of abuse. It is sad to say, but in the

"You may not understand her feelings, but that gives you no right or reason to blast her for saying something you don't get."

world we live in ladies are much more likely to have their physical safely violated.

Your wife is likely to make sure the house is locked up at night. She is more likely to want you to install a security system. A man is more likely to buy a gun or have his baseball bat located in a place for him to "deal" with a potential intruder. We men are no more physically prepared to deal with a bad guy than women; we just have our pride.

It's important we do what we can to help our ladies feel safe. Make sure you never make fun of them for wanting to feel safe.

You make sure the doors are locked and get a security system if she feels the need to have one.

Emotional Security

Another area she needs to be secure in is her emotions. She needs to know she is safe when she communicates to you about her feelings.

You may not understand her feelings, but that gives you no right or reason to blast her for saying something you don't get.

When my wife and I were first married, she could not handle any kind of verbal conflict with me. She was emotionally fragile and I was not sensitive to her at all. She really believed we were headed for divorce any time we got into any argument.

Relational Security

First, she needs to know beyond a shadow of a doubt that you are monogamous. You make it clear to her verbally and through your actions you are a one-woman man and she is your one woman.

Next, she needs to know you are willing to fight for her love and affection. You are willing to date her and do what it takes to have a great friendship with her. She needs to know you will fight for her if you needed to.

She needs to know you will protect her from other relationships that might hurt her. If she feels under attack or harm from anyone, she needs to know you will step in and protect her, especially from family. There are even times you may protect her from your children, from your parents, or from hers.

We men do not take on the responsibilities of the relationships in our home, mom does. Your wife intuitively needs to know everyone living under her roof is getting along. The more people living in your home, the more stress is on her. The more children you have, the more relational stress is on mother. You sometimes need to protect her by not allowing "extras" to live in your house. Dr. Talley actually has a math equation that helps us understand the amount of relationships that must function for there to be peace in HER home.

$R = N$ squared $- N \div 2$

$R =$ The Number of Relationships

N = The Number of People

Example: Husband + Wife + 4 kids --- N = 6

R = 6 x 6 = 36 – 6 = 30 ÷ 2 = 15

R = 15

In a home with six people, there are fifteen inter-personal relationships that must get along.

For fun, move her parents in with your family and the eldest child's girlfriend or boyfriend.

Now we have a total of nine people living in the house.

R = 9 x 9 = 81 – 9 = 72 ÷ 2 = 36

R= 36

In a home of nine people, there are thirty-six inter-personal relationships that must get along.

Financial Security

Again, you don't have to be rich. You don't have to keep up with the Joneses. You simply need to earn more than your family needs to spend.

When money is tight, you take the calls from bill collectors. You juggle what you must to take care of things. You make the tough calls when you have to tell your family it's time to loose cable TV and the Gold's Gym membership.

She needs to know you are willing to do whatever it takes to provide for her and her children.

This does not mean your wife can't work outside the home, you just do everything you can to help her not have to, if she does not want to.

In most cases, if you take care of her security, she will take care of your need for significance.

Chapter 19

PhD in Spouse and Children

Greg C. Gunn was a businessman in Oklahoma City. He and his wife Rhonda started a ministry in 1997 called Family Vision Weekend. They realized there was a great disconnect for most men when it came to their families. We men have a great ability to make a strategy for

winning in sports, hunting, business, and even war. The great disconnect is the fact that we never even think about a strategy for victory as husbands and fathers.

Before any of their seven children were born, early on in their marriage, Greg and Rhonda set out on a mission to learn what makes for good parents and healthy Christian children. They spoke to teachers, family counselors, pastors, relatives, and friends. The overall consensus from all of them is that you can do everything right as parents and still end up with a lukewarm family and messed up kids. As

"What good would it do for you to win the entire world to Christ and lose your own children to the darkness?" - -Greg Gunn

a matter of fact, they discovered the American family "bar" was set pretty low. Parents considered themselves successful as long as their kids graduated from high school without having a drug or alcohol problem, without getting or getting someone pregnant, without getting an STD, and at least attending church with them most of the time. The words they heard over and over were your spouse and children are just "The luck of the draw".

"You mean you can do everything right and end up with a horrible family?"

"Are you people saying parents have no effect on the outcome of the family?"

"Do coaches and CEO's have an effect on the outcome of the game or the business?"

I think we would agree that when the board of directors hired Jack Welch to lead GE, they assumed his leadership skills would make a difference in profits for the company.

Bob Stoops is the current head coach for the University of Oklahoma. The college pays him over $4,000,000.00 a year. Do you think the people that hired him crossed their fingers and said "I hope we get lucky this year with good players!"? Year in and year out, they are expecting Coach Stoops to have a winning effect on the games.

Greg and Rhonda refused to believe in this "luck" driven outcome for the children of our future. They set out on a mission to do spouse and children on purpose. They were talking to a pastor friend of theirs who, in passing, mentioned they will be out of town the coming weekend to do their annual family goal setting weekend. "Whaaat?!? Did you say you go away for a weekend and make a plan for your family for the following year?" Their friend explained what they do and why. A few weeks later, the Gunns went away on their first "Family goal setting weekend."

They spend the weekend in prayer and scripture asking God to lead them, so they can properly lead their family. They came across Jeremiah 35. It's the story of the Rechabite family. Their great, great grandfather wrote down the basic rules & guidelines the family was to live by. He told them to be herdsmen, to live in tents, to never own land, and to not drink wine. Two hundred years later, this family was still living by this code and when the Babylonians came from the east and wiped out the nation of Israel, the Rechabites rolled up their tents and herded their sheep to Egypt. When the dust settled, they were able to move back home as easy as they left.

Greg and Rhonda put two and two together and made a connection. Coaches and business leaders have a written plan they follow. They also have a written purpose, a written vision, a written mission, written core values, and written goals.

With the help of Mark and Kerri Naylor, a couple in their Sunday School class, Family Vision Weekend Ministries was born.

(You can Google Family-ID, Greg C. Gunn, or Family Vision Ministries to find out more.)

"What good would it do for you to win the entire world to Christ and lose your own children to the darkness?" ---Greg C. Gunn

Chapter 20

Make Her Your Best Friend!

Friendship is extremely important. John Gottman, a marriage researcher, says the number one thing husbands and wives both want from each other is being each other's number one best friend.

For some reason no one prepares us for friendship and in our culture we are taught that physical intimacy comes first and if we like that part, we can move forward with marriage and babies.

Dr. Talley teaches how important friendship is. In years past, there was something they called "courting." Courting was not what we call dating. It was the process of becoming friends and getting to know one another as friends. It is vitally important to your marriage that you begin your relationship with friendship, a genuine like for each other's company.

"There is no more lovely, friendly, and charming relationship, communion, or company than a good marriage."
–Martin Luther

Think about your best male friend now or your

best friend growing up. You like that person and at any given time, you have no expectation of them for anything. If the person does not deliver on an expectation, you are quick to forgive and forget. The same generosity of grace is sent back your direction when you drop the ball. At the end of the day you accept and like each other no matter what. Furthermore, you like to hang out together doing things, or not doing anything.

ALLSBURY FAMILY LAW

We have a rule in our house for our five kids and for each other. WE WILL TREAT EACH OTHER BETTER THAN OUR BEST FRIEND. It's not only a rule, we have passed a law and it's the most important law in our house.

Summer about five years ago I was in my office working and heard a commotion in the living room. I peeked in just in time to see my thirteen-year-old son throw a book at my (then) sixteen-year-old son's head. It was an actual fight. I was too late to see the punches that were exchanged. When the boys noticed me, the battle ended. I asked them to step into my room. "What on earth are you two fighting about?" Austin, the elder, stood quietly in the doorway as Avery spoke, "You told me to take the trash out. When I was outside Austin came into the living room, sat where I was sitting, took my pillow and changed the channel. He wouldn't move…" I silently asked the Lord for wisdom and then began to speak. "Avery, what if you left the room, came back, and your best friend, Chris, were sitting in your seat with your pillow and changed the channel? How would you have reacted?" Avery: "I would have grabbed another pillow and watched what he was watching." Then, "Austin, what if your friend, Ben, walked in the room and announced you had taken his seat, pillow, and changed the channel. How would you have reacted?" Austin: "Dad, I would have jumped up and apologized…" That's all it took for them to get the message. They smiled and walked out.

The rule applies to me as well. I simply must treat my bride better than my best friend, my neighbor, or my client.

If she really is your best friend, it is easy.

Shoulder to shoulder or face to face…

Girlfriend stuff and boyfriend stuff is different. We boys do things shoulder to shoulder with our friends. There is not a lot of eye contact and we don't talk about feelings. We shoot something, drink something, throw something, or catch something. When we talk about life, we do better driving someplace in a car or while engaging in manly activities.

My wife can get together with a few gals and sit around a small table, look into each other's eyes, and talk about relationships, feelings, and issues for hours. This only happens in a man's world if he is in trouble.

Part of your learning to become her friend is caring about how friendship happens in her world: talk to her less shoulder-to-shoulder and more face-to-face; listen without fixing the problem coming out of her mouth.

As I talk to you about this, it sounds so simple. It's not easy for us. We often have to bite our tongue until it bleeds. Allow her to "ground her capacitor" from her mouth to your ears. Be her best friend.

Mark Driscoll of Mars Hill Church in the great Northwest has a sermon series called Real Marriage. He tackles the friendship topic head-on. He and his wife, Grace, read all or part of 187 Christian books on marriage and relationships. They discovered that none of them really addressed the subject. How could friendship, the foundation of marriage, be missed by so many?

Mark tells the story of the greatest theologian of the Middle Ages, Martin Luther, and his wife, *Katharina von Bora*. Theirs is not the average story of romance. Luther was busy railing against the Catholic Church in his writings. One pamphlet in particular was about the fallacy of priest and nuns being celibate. He wrote about how the Bible does not celebrate the celibate and how it encourages marriage and children. A group of twelve nuns at a monastery in Germany read his writings, decided he was correct, and wanted to leave the convent, get married, and have kids. They wrote letters to him and asked for help. One Easter celebration in the early 1500's Luther used a caterer and twelve fish barrels to smuggle each of the unhappy nuns out of the monastery. Eleven of the twelve found husbands not long after their escape. Katharina von Bora never did. They say she was ugly and unpleasant to be around. She confronted Martin about her situation being in limbo between Nun and Wife. She told him it was his responsibility to marry her and eventually, he did. *He was actually a forty-year-old virgin.* They were first roommates and then became friends over time. She helped him make his house a comfortable home and started feeding him properly. They began to like each other, love each other, and eventually had six children together.

Martin Luther once wrote, "There is no more lovely, friendly, and charming relationship, communion, or company than a good marriage."

No matter how your marriage started, it's not too late to become friends.

When Dr. Talley counsels married couples who have separated, he instructs them to become reconciled as Christian friends. He will tell them that they may or may not ever get back together as a married couple, but, if he has anything to do with it, they will become friends. Friendship is the best place to start, especially for the benefit of your children.

If you can become friends, you have a chance to become more over time.

Treat each other better than your best friend.

Be her best friend.

78270130R00082

Made in the USA
San Bernardino, CA
04 June 2018